རྒྱ་ཆེན་དང་འོད་ཀྱ
ང་ཀྱི་སྣང་བ།

Vast and Radiant

སྨུག་གཟིག་

A series of Poems
By Tagzig

Prologue

The Mystical Stream: Awakening to Our True Nature

These pages hold the **essence of the world's most spiritually advanced traditions**. They'll open portals of consciousness, helping you not just discover who you are, but also **expand your being**. You'll attain profound experiences of your own essence through the wonder of the simple and direct.

Throughout human history, **mysticism has been the silent river nourishing the roots of all great spiritual traditions**. Beyond doctrines, rituals, and cultural forms, it's the mystical impulse—the yearning for a direct encounter with the sacred, the infinite, the essence of being—that has shaped civilizations, inspired art, and transformed lives. This drive connects humanity's deepest spiritual quests, from the **Advaita Vedanta**'s pursuit of **Brahman** to the **Dzogchen**'s realization of **Rigpa**, the **Mahamudra**'s direct perception of mind's nature, the **Tao**'s alignment with universal flow, and the **Christian mystics'** union with the Divine Ground, or the **Sufi's** experience of **Wahdat al-Wujud**.

However, mysticism isn't a privilege reserved for saints or sages. It's a **universal dimension of human experience**, woven into existence itself. From the deserts where early Christian hermits listened to the wind, to the mountain caves where Tibetan yogis sought the mind's luminous nature; from the poetry of wandering Sufi mystics to the silent Zen monasteries, seekers have found a truth that transcends language, dogma, and division. Their testimonies converge: **at the heart of existence lies an**

immediate, luminous, and accessible reality for all who dare to look inward. This shared recognition of an ultimate, unitive truth is where diverse mystical paths meet, revealing their underlying unity.

In every era, mystics remind us that the deepest answers aren't found in external achievements or fleeting possessions, but in the **rediscovery of our own essence**. Beneath the surface of our restless minds and fragmented societies, there exists a profound unity—a **pure being, an unlimited consciousness**—that connects us to one another, to nature, and to the great mystery we call God, Tao, or Rigpa. **Mystics connect with this Universal Intelligence by dissolving the illusion of separation**, often through intense contemplative practices, deep surrender, and a purification of perception that allows the inherent divine presence to shine through. They don't just believe in God; they experience being one with the Divine Ground, the infinite ocean of being.

The importance of mysticism in human life cannot be overstated. It offers **solace in uncertainty, healing in moments of despair, and wisdom in times of confusion**. More than a philosophy or a practice, it's a way of seeing—an invitation to experience life not as a problem to be solved, but as a **miracle to be lived**. It calls us to awaken to what has always been present: the infinite within the finite, the sacred in the everyday, the light at the center of our being.

This book is an invitation to rediscover that living source, to listen to the voices of mystics across cultures and centuries, and to recognize that their journey is, in truth, our own. In a world that yearns for connection, depth, and authenticity, the mystical path doesn't offer an escape, but a return—to ourselves, to others, and to the heart of all things.

The Natural Path of Awakening

In this time of confusion and inner noise, where the mind frantically searches for answers in a thousand directions, **Dzogchen** reveals itself as the most direct, naked, and luminous essence of awakening. Not as a system of beliefs, nor even as a philosophy, but as the **real possibility of recognizing what has always been present**: the pure nature of the mind, called **Rigpa**.

To dwell in **Rigpa** is to dwell in the silent core of reality. It's not about evading life, but seeing through it, without distortion. What's so special about Dzogchen? Its **radical simplicity**: nothing to build, nothing to reject, just discovering the clear, empty, and luminous presence that we already are. This non-conceptual directness is what links it to the **Advaita Vedanta**'s immediate realization of Brahman, the **Mahamudra**'s recognition of mind's true face, and the **Tao**'s effortless flow. It's the ultimate mystical shortcut to realizing the Universal Intelligence.

The path unfolds into two great avenues:

- **Trekchö**: the "total cutting through" of mental veils, which introduces us to profound insight through absolute rest in the essence.
- **Tögal**: the direct vision that, working with the natural light of the body and consciousness, leads to the

manifestation of clear visions and the extraordinary possibility of the **Rainbow Body (Jalü)** realization.

This **Rainbow Body (Jalü)** is not a symbolic myth. It has been lived and manifested by Tibetan masters like **Shardza Tashi Gyaltsen**, and sustained in living lineages such as that of Salza Rinpoche, whose life was an embodiment of Dzogchen's experiential wisdom. The dissolution of the physical body into light at death isn't a miracle; it's a **natural consequence of a life lived in Rigpa**, in perfect harmony with the Universal Intelligence, just as Christian mystics spoke of deification or Sufis of complete annihilation *(fana)* in God.

In times when spirituality is diluted by superficial discourse, preserving Tibetan mysticism isn't nostalgia; it's the **defense of a millennial lineage of direct experience of the Real**. Mysticism doesn't belong to one culture, but to the **universal heart of the human being** that yearns for freedom, clarity, and compassion. This profound common ground is what allows the insights of Dzogchen to resonate with truth-seekers across all faiths and philosophies.

This book is an invitation to remember what was never truly forgotten, to look inward not as an effort, but as an immense softness. May every word awaken in you the silent certainty that **you already are what you seek**.

Samaya

To Kuntu Zampo, the everlasting goodness.

To my mentors.

To the Masters of the past, present and future.

I bow down, pay homage.

Timeless freedom, abiding with no objective, luminous awareness shines forth, when pure nature is recognized, speechless knowing .

All enlightened qualities arise in effortless remaining, thus this realty is transcended. All pain is recognized as pure energy, just be, let go of your self into utterly unpolarized Awareness.

Indestructible space that transcends all concepts, can only be known in total freedom, consciousness is dissolved, any sensation or thoughts is recognized as a pure manifestation of this thoughtless non conceptual reality beyond dualism, nor can be defined or explained but only experienced.

Let go of everything and you will certainly be free, let go into this luminous experience. Then peace, love, compasión , and joy will arise naturally in effortless perfection.

སྟག་གཟིག་

Tagzig

འགྲོ་བ་ཐམས་ཅད་ཀྱི་གཏན་ཚིག།

འགྲོ་བ་ཐམས་ཅད་སྐྱིད་པ་དང་ཡིད་འོང་ཐུགས་རྗེ་འཕེལ་ཤོར།
གཟིགས་མེད་གྲོལ་ཤོར་ནི་འདི་རིག་པ་འོད་དཔག་གཏིང་ཟབ་ཏུ་གསལ་ཤོར།

གཡོ་བའི་སེམས་ཞི་བར་འགྲོལ། མཚོ་དང་མ་བཅོས་གཏིང་ཟབ་ཏུ་འོག་འབྱུང་།
རྣམ་པ་དང་བཅོག་མ་གཡོ་བའི་མཚོའི་གསལ་བ། འཏུལ་མེད་དང་སྨོན་འགྲོ་དང་བཅུག་མེད།

གཟིགས་མེད་རིག་པ་དང་མཚོའི་དག་བ། འགྲོ་བ་ཐམས་ཅད་ངོ་བོ་གསལ་ཤོར།
འཚོ་བ་ཡང་དག་པར་གནས་ཚུལ་ཏུ་ཡོད་ཤོར།

ཉམས་མེད་དང་དག་བ་དང་བརྟེན་ནས་རིག་པ་རང་བཞིན་གཏིང་ཏུ་གསལ་ཤོར།
འགྲོ་བ་ཐམས་ཅད་ཀྱི་དམ་ཚིག་དང་འོད་འོད་གསལ་ཤོར།

Prayer for All Beings

May all beings be happy,
May their hearts awaken to boundless peace.
May the veils of confusion dissolve,
Revealing the pure light of their true nature.

May the restless mind find stillness,
Like a clear lake, reflecting the open sky.
May the waves of thought return to the ocean,
Their essence never apart from the depths.

May every breath be a step toward freedom,
Every moment a gateway to boundless clarity.
May all beings realize their intrinsic perfection,
And dance in the radiance of their own awareness.

May suffering cease, may joy arise,
May the vast, open heart of wisdom shine,
Unfettered, unclouded, forever free—
May all beings know their true nature.

ཧུས་མེད་ཀྱི་རང་དབང་། དམ་ཅན་གྱི་དོན་མེད་པར་བཞག་པ།
འོད་གསལ་གྱི་རྣམ་ཤེས་འོད་འབར་བ། རང་བཞིན་དག་པ་ཡིས་རིག་ནས་
སྐད་མེད་ཀྱི་ཤེས་པ་གསལ་བ།།
རིགས་ཀུན་ལས་འབྱུང་བའི་ཡོན་ཏན་རྒྱལ་མར་བཞག་པར་འབྱུང་བ།
དེ་ནས་རྣམ་དག་གི་ཆོས་ཉིད་ལས་འཁྲོས།
སྤྱུག་བསྒྱུལ་ཡང་ནམ་རང་འགྱུར་གྱི་ནུས་ཤུགས་སྐྱེ་རིག་པ།
གང་ཡང་མི་བཞག་པར་གནས།
བདག་སེལ་ནས་མཉམ་པ་མེད་པའི་རང་རྒྱལ་གྱི་རྣམ་ཤེས་ནུས་མེད་ཧུ་བ
ཞིག།
མཚན་མེད་པའི་དབྱིངས་ནི་རྟོགས་པ་ཡང་མི་འགྲིམ་གྱིས་མཐོང་བ་དང་།
ཤེས་པ་མི་ཡོངས་པས་བཟློག་པར་འགྲོ།
ཚོར་བ་དང་རིག་པ་ཡང་དག་པའི་རང་བཞིན་གྱི་སྤྱོད་པ་སྐྱེ།
བདེ་ཆེན་མཚན་མེད་པ་ཧུས་མེད་ཀྱི་རང་བཞིན་རང་གིས་མཐོང་བ་རྒྱ་ཡི
ན།།
ཐོག་མར་གང་ཡང་སྔོན་ལས་བཞག་པ་སྤངས་ནས་
ཡང་དག་པའི་རང་དབང་ལ་འཇུག་པ་འགྲུབ།
འོད་གསལ་གྱི་ཉམས་སྐྱོང་ཡང་སྤངས་ན། ཞི་བ། བརྩེ་བ། ཐུགས་རྗེ།
དགའ་བ་ལས་རྒྱས་པར་མི་ལྷར་བྱས་ན་བྱུང་གི་ཙང་།།

The Luminous Recognition of Mind

To recognize **rigpa** is to turn toward the uncontrived essence of awareness—vast, untainted, beyond thought. It is the quiet unfolding of what has always been, the effortless arising of truth when all grasping ceases.

No effort constructs it, no analysis reveals it, no seeking attains it. It is only known when everything is left **as it is**—the rippling mind settling into its own reflection, awareness resting within itself, clear and unmoving like a sky untouched by clouds.

For some, the realization dawns suddenly, breaking through in an instant like sunlight piercing mist. For others, the unfolding is gentle—a centering, an anchoring, and then, like a river merging into ocean, all distinctions dissolve into the expanse.

Yet whether swift or slow, the path is the same: not in words, nor thought, but in the **direct encounter** with presence—beyond concept, beyond effort, beyond the illusions of past and future.

Nothing was ever missing. Nothing was ever apart. One simply **sees**. In this seeing, there is no one who sees—only the luminous vastness, awake and whole. This is **the Great Perfection**—self-arising, timeless, pure. This is the **unfolding of mind's true nature**. This is home.

Pure Being

Rigpa, true nature of the mind, sometimes referred to here as *pure being*. The key idea is that this nature is already complete; there is nothing to add or improve. It just needs to be recognized. Once we see this, we can rest in that recognition, without overthinking or trying to analyze it. It's like the sunrise—no matter how much we try to control or understand it, it just happens naturally. Similarly, the nature of our existence is perfect in itself, and the best way to experience it is to simply let it be. By realizing this, we stop searching for something outside of ourselves and find peace in what already is perfect.

By recognizing one's purity, positive qualities such as love, peace, and compassion manifest effortlessly. This recognition is not achieved through reasoning but through direct, non-conceptual experience, letting everything be as it is, like a pond without ripples.

The mental habits and repetitive behaviors we develop over time can be limiting. These patterns, stemming from an unconscious self, can prevent us from reaching our true potential and experiencing life fully. Through mindfulness practice and self-knowledge, we can free ourselves from these limitations, achieving greater freedom and authenticity in our lives. With awareness we see it as observing from the roof of a building.

Introd uction to the Nature

of the

Mind

Both Mahamudra and Dzogchen are ancient meditation traditions within Tibetan Buddhism that emphasize the direct realization of the mind's true nature. However, they approach this realization through slightly different methods and philosophical frameworks.

The aim is to ultimately bring practitioners to a direct, non-dual experience of the mind's nature. However, Mahamudra typically involves a more gradual progression through various stages of meditation, while Dzogchen emphasizes the immediate recognition of the mind's intrinsic nature. Despite these differences, both traditions share a common goal: the realization of the mind's inherent purity, clarity, and non-duality.

Recognizing the true nature of reality and ourselves is essential. In both traditions, the direct experience of this nature leads to liberation and enlightenment, transcending the dualities and conceptual fabrications that obscure our true essence. As practitioners rest in the natural state of mind, they discover a profound sense of peace, clarity, and interconnectedness, reflecting the boundless nature of their true being.

Trekchö Practice

Trekchö means "cutting through" and refers to the practice of cutting through all mental elaborations and concepts to recognize the essential nature of the mind. By letting everything be as it is, one fully trusts in this stillness, a peace that arises naturally and radiant light.

Rigpa in the Dzogchen Tradition

Overview

The Dzogchen tradition of Tibetan Buddhism centers around the concept of Rigpa (རིག་པ་), often translated as "knowledge" or "pristine awareness." Rigpa is the direct experience of the ultimate ground of existence, distinguishing it from the ordinary mind (Sems, སེམས་), which is characterized by dualistic perception and conceptual obscurations.

- **Rigpa represents pure, non-dual awareness**, free from conceptual limitations.
- **Sems**, in contrast, is **deluded awareness**, entangled in **thoughts, emotions, and conditioned perception**.
- The **Dzogchen path** guides practitioners from **Sems (ordinary mind) to Rigpa (awakened awareness).**

The **recognition of Rigpa** is described as **"knowledge of the ground" (Gzhi, གཞི་)**, linking it to the **fundamental nature of reality**. Its realization equates to **understanding ultimate truth.**

The Transformative Benefits of Spirituality

Spirituality is more than belief—it is the deep unfolding of presence, the silent recognition of interconnectedness, and the gateway to inner freedom. Across traditions, teachings, and lifetimes, it has offered seekers a profound sense of peace, clarity, and joy—illuminating paths once shrouded in uncertainty. It is not merely an abstract philosophy, but a lived experience, enriching every aspect of existence.

Through spirituality, individuals awaken to **the vast expanse of awareness**, where resilience is cultivated, compassion arises effortlessly, and life is met with wisdom rather than reaction. It is a return to the simple truth: **e**verything is impermanent, yet everything is sacred.

རྫོགས་ཆེན་ལམ་མེད་དང་མངོན་སྤྱོད། — Dzogchen as a Direct Path Beyond Striving

While Dzogchen is sometimes referred to as a **"direct path" or "swift path"**, it **fundamentally emphasizes the absence of a conventional, step-by-step path to enlightenment**.

- The **ultimate result—realization of our true nature—is already inherently present** from the very beginning.
- **Dzogchen practice is not about striving to attain something new** but **recognizing and resting within the already existing perfection.**
- It is about **returning to our natural, unaltered state of being**, free from **motivated confusions of the ordinary mind.**
- This perspective aligns with the insight: > *"No Path, Just Resting—There is no path to walk or steps to take—only resting in the mind's nature as it is."*

རྫོགས་ཆེན་གཞུང་དང་རང་བྱུང་གཏིང་ཟབ།

Effortlessness and Non-Meditation in Dzogchen

The notion of **effortlessness (rtsol med, རྩོལ་མེད་)** is **central to Dzogchen's self-understanding.**

- The practice involves a **fundamental shift from "doing" to "being"**.

- **Resting in the natural state of mind** without **willful striving or manipulation.**
- Dzogchen emphasizes **"non-meditation" (bsgom med, བསྒོམ་མེད་)**—not opposed to action, but rather an **inner disposition of effortless spontaneity**.
- **Striving for a particular outcome or trying to "fix" the mind** can **obscure the inherent perfection already present.**
- The key is to **allow awareness to reveal itself naturally,** without **interference from conceptual striving.**

This principle is captured in the statement: > *"Nothing to Fix, Nothing to Chase—When striving ceases, clarity unfolds effortlessly."*

Inner Peace

Mysticism, at its core, is the art of letting go —the ability to rest in life's unfolding with grace, and trust in Pure Being. No longer burdened by attachment or fear, the mind discovers its natural stillness. Even amid chaos, a sense of calm remains.

Through practices such as meditation and mindfulness, individuals cultivate emotional stability. They learn to release negativity, allowing peace to arise effortlessly. They gain clarity on life's deeper purpose, stepping beyond doubt into fulfillment.

True peace is not the absence of difficulty—it is the unshakable presence of wisdom, allowing the heart to remain open in any storm.

Compassion and Understanding

Spirituality dissolves barriers between self and other. It nurtures the ability to see beyond superficial conflicts, revealing the essence of interconnectedness.

- **Forgiveness becomes possible**—not as an act of approval, but as a release from suffering.
- **Empathy deepens**—not through effort, but through recognition.
- **Relationships transform**—as love is no longer conditional, but boundless.

The awakened heart no longer asks, *"Who deserves my kindness?"* It simply radiates understanding, offering healing without demand.

The Dzogchen View: Compassion as the Basis of Enlightened Activity

In Dzogchen, it is taught that enlightened activity arises from compassion rather than from structured practices of accumulation or purification. The emanation of Nirmanakayas—physical manifestations of Buddhas—is said to emerge precisely from this boundless compassion. Their sole purpose is to benefit sentient beings, appearing naturally as circumstances demand.

This reveals the unity of wisdom and compassionate action. There is no separation between realization and its expression. The empty clarity of rigpa effortlessly manifests as responsive care, adapting to the needs of each situation without calculation or hesitation.

The Union of Wisdom and Compassion

Effortless recognition of rigpa brings forth wisdom, and wisdom naturally expresses itself as compassion. This is the heart of Dzogchen and Mahamudra—an uncontrived, spontaneous responsiveness that does not require effort or intention.

There is no need to fabricate compassion, nor to seek it through external means. It is already present, waiting to be revealed through the direct recognition of awareness. This understanding shifts the spiritual path from striving to resting in what has always been.

Liberation is not a distant goal but an effortless recognition of the unity of being. Compassion is not a separate achievement but the living radiance of awakened mind. In this recognition, there is no division, only the boundless responsiveness of clarity and love.

Beyond Ordinary Bliss

Unlike worldly happiness, which depends on external conditions, Dzogchen bliss arises from **the natural radiance of awareness**. It is **self-existing**, not produced by effort or external stimuli. This bliss is **inseparable from emptiness**, meaning it is not a fixed state but an expression of the **spontaneous presence (lhun-drub)** of rigpa.

Bliss and the Path of Great Perfection

Dzogchen emphasizes **effortless recognition** rather than striving for altered states. While bliss may arise, the true goal is to **rest in the natural state**, allowing all experiences—blissful or otherwise—to **self-liberate** without attachment.

Gratitude is the alchemy of perspective—the shift from lack to abundance, from discontent to appreciation. A spiritual life is not measured by external successes but by the ability to find joy in the ordinary.

- The glow of sunrise.
- The laughter of a loved one.
- The quiet hum of the wind through trees.

When gratitude becomes a way of being, **joy becomes effortless**.

གཙང་མ་ཡོངས་སུ་གཟིགས་པ།

གསོལ་མདོ་འགྲོ་བ། དཀོན་མཆོག་འཚོལ། འཁོར་བ་ནང་སྡིག་ཡོད། ཁྲིད་ནང་གསལ་བའི་འོད། ལོ་ཏོས་འཛིན་མེད་སྐྲོབས།

སྣ་རང་གཉིས་མེད། སྣང་བའི་ངང་དུ། བག་ཆགས་མེད་པའི་རང་བཞིན། ཕྱིའི་རང་བཞིན་གང་རིག་དང་། ལོ་ཏོས་འགྲོ་བའི་མེད་པ།

ངོ་བོ་གསལ་བའི་དཔེ་སྐྲོན། བརྗོད་མེད་མངོན་སངས། མི་དགོས་མེད་ནང་གི་གཞི། འཁྲུལ་བ་མེད། དབང་ཆེན།

འདི་དག་སྐྲོབས་ཆེན་འདུག སྲིད་པའི་འགྱུར་ལ་མེད། དབྱེ་མེད་རང་བཞིན་གི་བཞུགས། རང་འགྲོ་མེད་པ། སྟོང་རྩལ།

ཁྲུད་ཆོས་བསླབ་པ་མེད། ཆོས་འཁོར་མེད་པ། བདག་གི་ངོ་བོ་གསལ། ལོ་ཏོས་མི་དགའ། གཙང་མ།

འོད་གསལ་བའི་གཙང་དག མི་དགོས་མེད་གྲོགས། ལོ་ཏོས་འབྱུང་བ། ཕྱི་གི་མི་གཡོ། འགྲོ་བའི་མེད་པ། དམ་ཚིག་བརྗོད།

བརྗོད་མེད་གྲོགས་ཆེན་པོ། ཕྱིའི་མེད་རང་བཞིན། ཕྱི་གཙང་མ་ཡོངས་སུ་གཟིགས། ཕྱི་འདུག་འོད་གསལ་གཞི།

The Jewel Unseen

We gather gold, we chase the stars, We measure worth in fleeting things, Yet beneath the noise, beyond the far, A silent light within us sings.

No fear to bind, no hope to chase, No tangled past, no yet-to-be, Here and now—the boundless space, The lotus blooms, untamed, set free.

What grasp can hold the open sky? What name can carve the nameless vast? The mind untroubled, pure and high, Is the only wealth that ever lasts.

No anger now, no sorrow's chain, No weight of thought, no need for more, Just rest—just be—beyond all gain, The endless sea, the open shore.

Creazy times

Stanza 1:

We chase the stock, the screen, the fleeting high, Build paper walls against an open sky. Forgetting this: the mind, clear, deep, unbound, The only treasure truly to be found.

Stanza 2:

No future fix, no pilgrimage afar, The freedom waits right here, just where you are. Fear's phantom touch, the weight of what we crave, The angry storm, confusion's churning wave—Dissolve like mist when sun (this knowing) breaks, Right now, this breath, is all it ever takes.

Stanza 3:

Be Lotus Born—unruffled, simply here, Abide in presence, let the path be clear. Leave the screen's glare, the city's frantic pace, Find refuge in a quiet, open space. Less digital noise, more earth beneath the feet, Where ancient knowing makes the now complete.

Stanza 4:

This timeless wisdom, simple, ever true, Lies waiting in the open heart of you. Value this mind, this presence, calm and vast, The only anchor built to truly last. Here, now, is freedom. Here, the search is done. Be still, and know: the many are the One.

Freedom from Attachments and Expectations

Expectation is the root of suffering—clinging to outcomes, chasing control, fearing change. Spirituality invites a different approach: trusting the flow of life, releasing attachment to identity, status, or validation.

- Instead of striving, one moves with the rhythm of existence.
- Instead of resisting change, one embraces impermanence as liberation.
- Instead of needing approval, one discovers self-sufficiency—content in the natural state.

From this freedom, life ceases to be an endless pursuit. It becomes a dance—unfolding, shifting, alive.

Meaningful Work and Purpose

Work, in its highest form, is not a duty—it is a calling. Spirituality infuses meaning into every action, transforming the ordinary into the sacred.

- Work is no longer just survival; it becomes a space for growth and learning.
- Purpose is not found in status but in alignment with values.
- Fulfillment emerges when one's efforts serve something greater than the self.

Each task, each moment, each creation becomes an offering—a devotion to presence, to integrity, to service

Respectful and Loving Relationships

True connection is built upon mutual respect, presence, and understanding. A spiritually awakened individual does not seek love as something to possess but as something to share.

- Communication is softened by kindness.
- Patience replaces frustration.
- Love becomes a force of inspiration, not expectation.

Relationships cease to be sources of stress; they become reflections of wisdom, supporting growth rather than constraining it.

The Final Realization: The Simplicity of Being

Spirituality, in its purest essence, is **the return to simplicity**. It strips away illusions, dissolves boundaries, and reveals the luminous truth: That fulfillment was never in the future—it was always here, in the depths of presence.

To live spiritually is to live fully, fearlessly, freely. Not by escaping life—but by embracing it completely.

The journey is not to attain, nor to seek. It is only to recognize— That liberation, joy, and peace were never outside us.

They have always been **within**.

Living a Spiritually-Enriched Life

Spirituality is not about forcing it—it's about recognition of your pure mind, transformation, and alignment. By embracing its wisdom, life becomes more peaceful, joyful, and meaningful. It awakens a deeper sense of purpose, guiding individuals toward true fulfillment.

Dzogchen: A Synthesis of Wisdom

Dzogchen, the *Great Perfection*, is neither a path nor a goal—it is the recognition of what has always been present. Its essence transcends ritual, discipline, and conceptualization, pointing directly to the luminous clarity of mind that remains untainted by thought, emotion, or grasping.

The Basis of Renunciation

Renunciation in Dzogchen is not about abandoning the world but releasing attachment to illusions. It is the **effortless letting go** of dualistic perception, freeing the mind from grasping at appearances as real. Nothing needs to be purified or transformed—only recognized as self-liberating in its own nature.

The Advantage of Liberation

Liberation (*moksha, kaivalya*) is not an achievement, but a return to one's primordial state—*rigpa*, the effortless awareness that transcends suffering, attachment, and limitation. Its fruits are spontaneous peace, boundless compassion, and the radiant bliss that arises when clinging dissolves.

The Great Bliss—Ananda

True bliss is not sensory pleasure but the joy of resting in the nature of mind. When striving ceases, awareness itself shines as *mahasukhā*, the great bliss beyond conditions. It is the warmth of uncontrived presence, the effortless smile of wisdom itself.

The View, Meditation, and Conduct

- **View:** The direct recognition of mind's true nature—pure, luminous, and empty of inherent existence.
- **Meditation:** Resting in awareness naturally, beyond effort, beyond striving. Thoughts arise and dissolve like waves in the ocean.
- **Conduct:** Compassionate action flows spontaneously, not imposed by rules but arising naturally from wisdom.

Mindfulness Today—A Gateway to Presence

In a world of distraction, mindfulness reconnects us to the immediacy of experience. It is not an effort, but a return—to direct perception, to effortless awareness, to the simple reality of the present moment.

The Path Beyond Striving

Patanjali's stages of meditation—from concentration (*Dharana*) to absorption (*Samadhi*)—reflect the gradual dissolution of separateness. But Dzogchen offers the *direct path*, cutting through concepts, guiding the practitioner to recognize the natural state in this very moment. You may say *Phat*! Cut ! Most practitioners need to cultivate the preliminary practices of compassion, refuge, purification , etc . Then we should cultivate *shine* , calm abiding.

Once we are introduced to our nature of pure mind we could just trust that essence of being in all our actions day and night .

Dzogchen is the flight of birds across the sky—**without traces, without paths, without struggle**. It is the awakening into the luminous expanse of awareness, the recognition that there was never anything to attain, only something to realize.

Let go. Rest in the natural state. Be free.

Awareness
Wisdom

The Four Gates to Wisdom

1. **Recognizing the Preciousness of Life** This existence is rare—a bridge between ignorance and awakening. Embrace it fully, walking the path of wisdom with intention.
2. **Living with Awareness of Impermanence** All things rise and fall like waves upon the shore. By accepting transience, you discover the depth of each moment.
3. **Understanding the Power of Karma** The universe reflects what is sown. Act with care, knowing that kindness and clarity create ripples beyond yourself.
4. **Breaking Free from Delusion** Attachment binds, yet surrender liberates. Rest in awareness, allowing confusion to dissolve into spacious presence.

By integrating these teachings into our lives, we can navigate the chaos of the world with greater ease, trust in the natural flow of life, and experience profound growth and peace.

རིག་པའི་སྙ་དང་འོད་གསལ་རང་བྱུང་།

— The Essence of Rigpa and Direct Recognition

A **direct recognition** of our true nature, our essence—an awareness that is luminous, boundless, and free from conceptual limitations. In Dzogchen, this is known as **Rigpa** (རིག་པ་), the pristine awareness that is **self-existing** and **spontaneously present**. It is beyond intellectual grasping, beyond effort, and beyond duality.

Rigpa: The Essence of Awareness

Rigpa is often described as:

- **Primordial purity** (Ka-dag, ཀ་དག་)—the fundamental emptiness of mind, free from obscurations.
- **Spontaneous presence** (Lhun-drub, ལྷུན་གྲུབ་)—the radiant clarity that naturally manifests without effort.

Unlike ordinary perception, which is clouded by habitual thinking, Rigpa, our pure being, nature of the mind, is **self-aware and reflexive**, shining like the open sky—vast, clear, and unobstructed.

Ka-dag is the essence, Lhun-drub is its dynamic display—the spontaneous, self-arising manifestation of wisdom and phenomena from the Ground (gzhi).

Natural Manifestation

Ka-dag is unchanging, Lhun-drub is alive, expressing itself naturally. Wisdom and appearances unfold effortlessly—not as a result of effort, but simply as they are.

Effortlessness as the Path

The practitioner does not need to strive to generate wisdom or purify the mind. Instead, by resting in the natural state, wisdom and compassion **arise spontaneously**, without interference.

Ka-dag and the Ground (Gzhi, གཞི་): The Foundation of Reality

The Ground (gzhi) in Dzogchen philosophy is described as empty, lacking inherent existence, and primordially pure.

Clarity (gsal ba / lhun grub): The Luminous, Knowing Aspect

If Rigpa were *only* emptiness, it would be a blank, inert void. But Rigpa is not inert; it is vibrantly alive, self-aware, and possesses an inherent capacity to know and to manifest. This is its **clarity** or **luminosity** (*gsal ba*). It's the knowing, cognizant aspect of the Ground.

This clarity is not a product of external factors or a result of mental effort. It is spontaneously present (*lhun grub*), an intrinsic luminosity that illuminates itself and all phenomena. It's the inherent awareness that allows experiences to arise, to be known, and to be perceived.

The Reflective Mirror. A mirror is empty of the images it reflects; it doesn't *become* the image. But it's not a mere blank wall. Its emptiness is precisely what allows it to *clearly reflect* any image that comes before it. Its clarity is its inherent capacity to manifest appearances. Without this clarity, despite its emptiness, it would be useless as a mirror.

The Sun's Radiance. The sun itself (like emptiness) is beyond form and grasp, but its very nature is to spontaneously radiate light and warmth (clarity). This radiance illuminates everything without being diminished or stained by what it illuminates.

The Indivisible Union (zung 'jug): Luminous Emptiness

The core of Rigpa is the **inseparability** of emptiness and clarity. They are not two separate things that somehow combine, but two facets of the *same* indivisible reality. One cannot exist without the other in Rigpa.

If you have clarity without emptiness, it's a fixed, reified consciousness, which is still subject to dualistic grasping. If you have emptiness without clarity, it's a sterile nothingness.

Rigpa is precisely the *knowing* of this inherent clarity that is empty of inherent existence, and this emptiness that is inherently clear and knowing. It's often called "luminous emptiness" or "empty luminosity" (*stong gsal dbyer med*).

The Fire. Fire (Rigpa) has two inseparable qualities: heat (clarity/luminosity) and formlessness (emptiness). You cannot have one without the other. You can't separate the heat from the fire, nor can you point to a "form" of fire that exists independently of its heat and light.

Why this matters in Dzogchen practice:

- **Avoiding Nihilism or Eternalism:** Emphasizing only emptiness can lead to nihilism (a belief in nothingness), while emphasizing only clarity/consciousness can lead to eternalism (a belief in a permanent, fixed self or entity). The union of both avoids these extremes, accurately reflecting the dynamic and unconditioned nature of reality.
- **Direct Introduction:** Dzogchen masters often use "pointing-out instructions" to directly introduce students to Rigpa. These instructions aim to cut through conceptual overlay and allow the student to *recognize* the mind's true nature as this luminous emptiness, rather than intellectually constructing it.
- **The Basis for Manifestation:** It is this luminous clarity within the empty ground that allows for the spontaneous manifestation of all phenomena, both pure (nirvanic) and impure (samsaric). The "play" or "energy" (*rtsal*) of Rigpa arises naturally from this indivisible unity.

In essence, Rigpa is not a vacant space, but an **aware, awake, and spontaneously radiant emptiness**—a dynamic and living ground that is the source of all appearance, yet remains utterly pristine and free.

The sky within, so vast and clear,

No cloud can stain, no passing fear.

A silent flame, a mirror bright,
Reflecting all, yet pure in light.

No journey needed, no far quest, Just
here, just now, in quiet rest.

The drop, the ocean, one embrace,
Awakening to boundless grace.

The river of thought, it flows and turns, But deep beneath, a still pool yearns. A diamond mind, though dust may cling, Its pristine light forever sings.

The whispered word, the silent call, A boundless garden, embracing all. You are the breath, the dawn's soft hue, The ancient, ever-shining new.

The world unfurls, a vibrant scene, Yet quiet wisdom lies between. A deeper current, soft and deep, While busy hours their vigil keep.

Find stillness there, a shining guide, Where all you seek has long resided.

The Ground (*gzhi*): The Primordial Purity of Being

In Dzogchen, the Great Perfection, the ultimate reality is not something to be created, achieved, or even cultivated, but rather **recognized**. This recognition points to the **Ground** (*gzhi*), our primordial state, the fundamental basis of all existence, both samsaric and nirvanic. The Ground is often described with three fundamental aspects: **Essence**, **Nature**, and **Compassion/Energy** (or Radiance). Here, we will delve into its Essence, focusing on the profound concept of *Ka-dag*.

The Essence of the Ground: Ka-dag – Primordial Purity

The **Essence** aspect of the Ground is characterized by **emptiness** and **primordial purity**

Empty of Inherent Existence: When we say the Ground is "empty" (*stong pa nyid*), it doesn't mean a void or nothingness in the nihilistic sense. Instead, it signifies that it is empty of *inherent, independent existence.* No phenomenon, no thought, no emotion, no aspect of reality possesses a fixed, solid, or self-existent nature. Everything is interdependent, arising in relation to other things. This emptiness is dynamic, not static.

The Unseen Mirror

The river of thought, it flows and turns,
A ceaseless current, a mind that yearns.
But deep beneath, a **still pool** lies,
Reflecting truth to inner eyes.

A **diamond mind**, though dust may cling, Its pristine light forever sings. No need to polish, no need to clean, It simply *is*, serene, unseen.

The whispered word, the silent call, A **boundless garden**, embracing all. You are the breath, the dawn's soft hue, The ancient, ever-shining new.

You are the **cloudless sky**, so wide, Where passing storms no trace can hide. The **unwritten page**, pure, vast, and free, The **mirror's clarity** — that's truly you.

The **blank canvas** of the mind, so wide, Where fleeting brushstrokes softly glide. A **pristine mirror**, clear and deep, Reflecting secrets it will keep.

The **cloudless sky**, untouched by storm, Holds every passing shape and form. A **river of thought** may flow and turn, But underneath, a **still pool** yearns.

No need to polish, no need to clean, The **diamond mind**, forever keen. You are the breath, the dawn's soft hue, The ancient, ever-shining new.

The Unwritten Page or the Blank Canvas. Imagine a perfectly blank, pristine page or a vast, untouched canvas. It's not "nothing," but it's empty of any pre-existing story, drawing, or defilement. Its emptiness is its potentiality – the capacity for any story to be written, any image to be painted, without ever staining the page itself. The page remains fundamentally pure, no matter what is inscribed upon it. Similarly, the Ground is the empty spaciousness that allows all phenomena to arise, without itself being defined or limited by them.

Primordially Pure (Ka-dag): This is the core insight. The Ground, in its very essence, is **primordially pure** (*ka-dag*). This purity is not something attained through purification practices, nor is it a state that fluctuates. It means that from the very beginning, from time immemorial, our ultimate nature has been utterly free from any defilement, obscuration, or contamination. It is beyond all conceptual limitations, dualistic constructs, and karmic imprints. It is inherently flawless and stainless, irrespective of what appears within it.

The Pristine Mirror or the Cloudless Sky. Consider a perfectly polished, ancient mirror. No matter what images it reflects – beautiful or ugly, clear or distorted – the mirror itself remains fundamentally spotless and clear. The reflections come and go, but the mirror's intrinsic clarity is never stained or altered. It doesn't need to be "cleaned" to be pure; it *is* pure.

Another powerful metaphor is the **Cloudless Sky**. The sky is always vast, open, and clear. Clouds (our thoughts, emotions, karmic obscurations) may appear, gather, and obscure the sun, making the sky seem dark or turbulent. But the clouds are transient; they are distinct from the sky itself. When they dissipate, the sky's inherent blueness and openness are revealed, not because it was "purified," but because its true nature was always pure, even when obscured. *Ka-dag* is this inherent, unalterable purity of the sky, even when the clouds seem to dominate.

The Unconditioned Nature of Ka-dag

Ka-dag represents the natural, unaltered base of being, utterly beyond all attempts to conceptualize or control reality.

Ka-dag represents the natural, unaltered base of being, utterly beyond all attempts to conceptualize, define, or control reality. It exists prior to any mental fabrication, any concept of "self" or "other," "good" or "bad."

Beyond Mental Grasp: Our ordinary mind operates through concepts, labels, and categories. It tries to grasp, analyze, and pin down reality. But *Ka-dag* is the very ground upon which these mental operations occur, and therefore it cannot be grasped *by* them. It is the subject, not the object. Any attempt to conceptualize it immediately misses its point, like trying to catch water with a sieve.

The Eye Seeing Itself. Just as an eye can see everything but cannot see itself directly without a mirror, our ordinary mind can perceive phenomena but cannot directly perceive its own ultimate nature, *Ka-dag*, through conceptual thought. It requires a different mode of knowing – direct recognition.

The Unaltered Base: *Ka-dag* is the state of our being before any "doing" or "becoming." It is our primordially pure state, utterly free from the beginning. This means that even now, amidst our confusion, our suffering, our thoughts and emotions, *Ka-dag* remains untouched, ever-present, and unblemished. It is our unconditioned self, the perfect foundation that needs no improvement.

Gold Amidst Impurities. Even if gold is mixed with various impurities, its intrinsic nature as gold never changes. The impurities can be removed, but the gold itself doesn't become "more gold"; it simply reveals its inherent golden quality. Similarly, our *Ka-dag* nature is like gold; it doesn't become purer through practice, but its primordial purity is revealed as obscurations are allowed to naturally dissolve.

In essence, *Ka-dag* is the radical understanding that we are, in our deepest core, already perfect, already awake, already pure. The Dzogchen path is not about reaching this state, but about recognizing it in every moment, allowing the inherent qualities of the Ground to naturally manifest. It is the foundational clarity that liberates us from the endless cycle of striving and becoming.

Ka-dag as the Essence of the Ground

Ka-dag is intimately linked to the **Essence** aspect of the Ground—it is **the unchanging purity**, beyond **mental constructs** and **conceptual barriers**.

Why Is Recognition of Ka-dag the Key to Liberation?

✔ **No Need to Fabricate or Purify** Liberation does not come from **striving** to purify or **improve** the mind. Rather, it comes from **recognizing the mind's original, untainted nature**.

✔ **Resting in the Natural State** By **simply resting** in **what already is**, wisdom arises naturally. **No rejection, no grasping—just presence.**

✔ **The Path of Great Ease** This is why Dzogchen is often called **"the path of great ease"**—it is **not about achieving**, but about **recognizing what is already perfect and complete**.

Direct Recognition vs. Intellectual Understanding

- **Conceptual knowledge** operates within dualities—self and other, subject and object.
- **Direct recognition** dissolves these boundaries, revealing the **inseparable unity** of emptiness and clarity.
- **Transmission** from a qualified Dzogchen master is essential—it offers a glimpse into our already awakened state, bypassing intellectual analysis.

The Path of Spontaneity

We need to go back to simplicity like children . When we trust pure, naturality arises. Dzogchen emphasizes **direct experience** over conceptual study. When one trusts pure being, he nature of the mind everything is transformed. This nature of being rebels itself, when we let go. A paradox, silence, and sudden insight we break through mental constructs. We recognize the **already perfected nature**—not through effort, but through **recognition.**

Enlightenment is not something to attain—it is something to realize. The light of awareness is already shining; we simply need to recognize it .Entering the Practice: Resting in Awareness

Let Go of Expectations

- Release all **ideas or anticipations** of how meditation **should unfold.**
- Simply **be here**, free from **striving to control the experience.**
- Rest **in the openness of the present moment.**

Open the Eyes Softly

- Keep the **eyes slightly open**, with a **soft gaze** resting in front.
- Do not **focus on anything specific**—let **the world come to you naturally.**
- If helpful, **start by looking downward softly,** allowing the **visual field to remain open.**

Observing the Play of Awareness

Noticing the Arising of Thoughts

- Allow **thoughts to arise naturally**, without **blocking** or **following** them.
- Observe thoughts **as they appear**, recognizing them as **spontaneous movements** of awareness.
- Ask: **Where do they come from?** They **simply arise**.

Witnessing Their Dissolution

- See how **thoughts fade away on their own**, dissolving **just as effortlessly** as they arose.
- Ask: **Where do they go?** They return to the **same quiet space** from where they came.
- Recognize **their insubstantial nature**, allowing them to **self-liberate**.

Resting in the Space Between Thoughts

- After a thought **passes**, allow yourself to **rest in the stillness** that follows.
- There is **no need to explain or analyze**—just **experience the spaciousness** of mind, **free of effort**.
- This **gap between thoughts** is the **pure presence** of Rigpa.

Union with the Divine – 5 A

Your Body: In the base posture of the 5 points: crossed legs, straight back, chin tucked in, chest open, hands in a position of equanimity.

Breathing: Naturally and, long deeply, or do a pranajama

Mind: Imagine and then leave everything as it is.

Ray of Light from God or Enlightened Beings: Pronounce the prolonged syllable "A" feeling the light of the universe from all beings of light, it could be Buddha or Jesus or any being with whom you have a connection.

Sphere of Light in the heart appears and radiates light: Pronounce the prolonged syllable "A," feeling how the light enters through your central channel, creating a sphere that forms in your heart and radiates light.

---

[1] The essence of this practice is the union with the divine being that lives within you. The word "guru," although used as the wise one, is also the spiritual teacher who helps you discover your divine or perfect nature (omniscience), your pure essence. In India, it is called Brahma, and in the tradition of Advaita Vedanta, there is a mantra called "Aham Brahmasmi." You may say the mantra of love, love, love, light inside of me, shines everywhere.

The Sphere in Your Heart Radiates Light through Your Central Channel: Continue pronouncing the prolonged syllable "A," now feeling how the sphere of light in your heart radiates light through your energy channels and chakras.

Radiate Light to all our Subchannels energy: Pronounce the prolonged syllable "A," feeling the sphere of light in your heart, how it radiates light through all your energy subchannels, throughout your entire energetic body.

Dissolve Your Body (Ego) into the All: While pronouncing the prolonged syllable "A," feel the sphere of light in your heart radiating light, expanding and dissolving your body into the infinite and luminous space.

Unified Experience: In spontaneous presence, there is no separation between the observer and the observed. This unified experience reflects the non-dual nature of reality.

Joy and Ease: This spontaneous state is one of joy and ease, where actions flow naturally from an open and relaxed mind. Longchenpa teaches that everything in its natural state is inherently perfect. Spontaneity emerges when we let go of striving and trust in this intrinsic perfection. Thoughts are like birds passing through the sky—they come and go, leaving the sky unscarred. Emotions are like the wind—fleeting and impermanent, never changing the nature of the air. The mind is like a vast mountain; thoughts are clouds passing by its peak without leaving a mark. Thoughts and feelings are like shadows—they move and shift but never alter the essence of the light. Emotions are like the weather—constantly changing, yet the sky remains unaltered.

Integration: Carrying Awareness Beyond Meditation

Rest in the Flow of Awareness

- Observe **each moment as naturally perfect**, requiring **no effort or action** from you.
- Stay in **this effortless awareness** for as long as it feels comfortable.

Ending the Meditation with Presence

- Take a **deep breath**, acknowledging the **natural flow of thoughts**.
- Carry this **sense of ease and spaciousness** into your **daily life**.

རིག་པའི་དགོན་མཆོག། — The Essence of This Practice

This **Dzogchen meditation** is not about **blocking thoughts** or **trying to change the mind**. Instead, it:

- **Reveals the natural, self-liberating quality** of thoughts and emotions.
- **Invites the practitioner to witness the perfection** of awareness **as it is**.
- **Dissolves the habitual tendency** to fixate on mental formations.
- **Allows effortless recognition of Rigpa**, the **intrinsic presence beyond concept**.

Embracing the Ocean of Rigpa: Navigating Daily Life with Dzogchen

Dzogchen, the Great Perfection, isn't just for formal medita

གཞུང་དང་སྦྱོན་འགྲོ། — Example of Everyday Integration

- **In stressful moments**, pause and observe emotions **without attachment.**
- **Before speaking**, allow a gap in awareness, letting clarity **emerge naturally**.
- **While walking**, notice the flow of experience, resting in **spontaneous presence**.
- Dzogchen does not impose a fixed meditation structure—it is about recognizing and resting in the **natural perfection already present.**

This practice is not about doing—it is about being. By simply resting, recognizing, and remaining present, practitioners **awaken to the ever-present luminosity** of awareness in all aspects of life

tion; it's a profound way to live every moment, transforming stress and ordinariness into opportunities for liberation. The core insight is to shift from **doing to being**—recognizing and resting in the natural perfection that's always present, even amidst life's turbulence. Think of it as allowing your mind to settle into its vast, open nature, much like a **cloudless sky** remains untouched by passing storms.

Emotions: Waves in the Ocean of Rigpa

Often, we perceive emotions as separate, powerful entities that overwhelm us. In Dzogchen, however, emotions are not external invaders but **waves in the vast ocean of Rigpa** itself. They arise, play, and dissolve within the boundless expanse of your awareness.

- **In Stressful Moments:** When an intense emotion hits—anger, anxiety, fear—don't try to suppress it or push it away. Instead, **pause and simply observe it as it arises**. Feel its raw energy in your body, acknowledge its presence, but don't get caught in its story. See it like a cloud forming, moving, and dissipating in the sky. Your awareness, your Rigpa, remains the vast, clear sky, utterly untouched and spacious. The wave might be powerful, but the ocean it arises from is infinitely vaster and always remains unchanged in its essence.
- **The Luminous Nature of Emotion:** Even the most challenging emotions are, at their core, **expressions of Rigpa's energy**. They are not inherently negative; it's our grasping or aversion that makes them problematic. When you rest in Rigpa, the energy of emotion is liberated into its clear, unconditioned nature, like a tangled knot unraveling into free-flowing thread.

Before Speaking: The Sacred Pause

Our words often spring from habit, conditioning, or reactivity. Dzogchen invites a profound shift:

- **Allow a Brief Gap:** Before responding or initiating speech, cultivate a brief, conscious **gap in your awareness**. It's like pressing a mental "reset" button. In that open space, just for a moment, simply rest. This isn't about thinking; it's about being.
- **Clarity and Natural Wisdom Emerge:** From this spaciousness, clarity and natural wisdom can spontaneously emerge. This "gap" invites **spontaneous presence**, preventing reactive, habitual speech and allowing your words to arise from a deeper, more authentic place. It's like a clear pool where reflections become sharp after the ripples subside.

While Walking: The Dance of Perception

Even simple movements become profound practices:

- **Rest in Spontaneous Presence:** As you walk, bring your attention to the flow of sensations and experiences. Notice the movement of your body, the contact of your feet with the ground, the sights, sounds, and smells around you. Don't label or analyze; simply allow perceptions to arise within your awareness.
- **All Arising Within the Luminous Field:** Every step, every sensation, every perception is not separate from you, but **arising within the luminous field of your awareness**. You are not merely observing; you are the awareness in which everything appears. It's like being the light that illuminates the path, rather than just the traveler on it.

The Effortless Path: Rest, Recognize, Remain

Dzogchen doesn't demand rigid meditation structures or elaborate techniques. Its essence is to **recognize and rest in the natural state—Rigpa—amidst all activities**, whether sitting, speaking, moving, or feeling. This practice isn't about effort or striving; it's about being fully present and allowing the inherent luminosity of awareness to shine through every aspect of life.

By simply resting, recognizing, and remaining present, you awaken to the **ever-present luminosity of awareness**. You discover that every moment—pleasant or stressful, profound or mundane—is an opportunity to return to your true nature. It's like finding that the **lamp** was always lit, even when you thought you were in darkness. The **diamond** was always there, just waiting for the dust to settle.

Emptiness and Luminosity: The Mirror Mind Analogy

Dzogchen **uses powerful analogies** to illuminate the **nature of awareness**.

1. The Mirror of Mind

- Just as a mirror effortlessly reflects images without attachment, mind reflects all thoughts, emotions, and experiences.
- The reflections do not alter the purity of the mirror itself—emphasizing non-clinging.

2. Spontaneous Liberation (Rang-grol, རང་གྲོལ་)

- Thoughts and emotions liberate themselves naturally when met without grasping or suppression.
- Illustrated through metaphors such as:
    - A snake effortlessly uncoiling itself.
    - A thief entering an empty house and finding nothing to steal.

འཁྲུག་འགྲོའི་བར་དོ།

དུས་རབས་འཁྲུག་འགྲོའི་གནས།
སྣང་བའི་བརྙན་གྱུ་འཁོར་འཁོར་བའི་འཁོར།
བརྗིད་པའི་སྒྲལ་འཕྲད་དུས་སྐོང་དག།
རྒྱ་ཆེའི་འཁྱིལ་བའི་འཕྲུལ་བའི་རྒྱལ།

དེ་རིང་གཅིག་པའི་རྗེས་སུ།
འདུལ་བའི་མོས་པ་རྒྱས་པའི་བསམ།
སེམས་དང་རང་རྒྱལ་འབར་བའི་སྒྲ།
གཅིག་ཏུ་སེམས་པའི་གཏིང་དུ་བསྟེན།

འགྲོ་མེད་པའི་འཁོར་ལོ།
གཏིང་དུ་མེད་པའི་རྒྱ་མཚོ།
དགའ་སྟོན་བཞིན་པའི་སྤྱོད་པ།
རྩེ་མོ་བཞིན་པའི་དབུས་གནས།

དངོས་སུ་དག་པའི་ངང་ལ་གནས།
འགྲོ་མེད་བྱུང་བ་མེད་པའི་བར་དོ།
རྒྱ་མཚོ་འཁྱིལ་བ་ལྟར།
ཡུལ་དང་འབྲེལ་བའི་གནས།

རྟོགས་པའི་སྒྲར་འཁྱིལ་བའི་མཐའ།
གཏིང་དུ་བཞིན་པའི་རྒྱ་མཚོ།
འཁོར་ལོ་འཁྲུལ་མེད་པའི་སྤྱོད།
དགའ་སྟོན་བཞིན་པའི་རྒྱ་མཚོ།

རྒྱ་ཆེར་འཕྲུལ་བའི་སྒྲོན་མ།
འཁོར་འཁྲུལ་འབྲུམ་བྱུང་བའི་སྤྱོད།
རྩེ་མོ་ལྟར་གྲུབ་པའི་རྒྱ་མཚོ།
གཏིང་དུ་འཁྱིལ་བའི་རྒྱ་མཚོ།

འཁོར་འཁྱིལ་དང་ལྡན་པའི་རྒྱ་མཚོ།
འཁྱིལ་བའི་དགའ་སྟོན་བཞིན་པའི་གནས།
དབྱིངས་གཅིག་དུ་གནས་པའི་གནས།
གཏིང་དུ་བཞིན་པའི་རྒྱ་མཚོ།

In the Midst of the

Whirl wind

In this age of flickering screens,
Of shattered moments and restless dreams,
We race on roads with no true end,
Chasing reflections, forgetting to bend.

But here, in the quiet folds of time,
A whisper rises, ancient, sublime—
"You are already whole, already bright,
A sun unclouded, a boundless light."

No need to mend, no need to chase,
No fractured self to rearrange.

Let go of striving, the ceaseless pace,
And find the stillness, vast and strange.

In the heartbeat of this rushing age,
Let the mind unfurl, let the thoughts engage,
Not as burdens, but as fleeting play,
Waves in an ocean, a timeless sway.

Each breath, a bridge, a gentle trace,
Each thought, a cloud in empty space.
Let the dance of life be free, unplanned,
Let the river flow, unheld, unspanned.

For in this fleeting, fractured sphere,
The open sky remains ever clear.
No path to walk, no race to run,
Just resting in the light of the primordial sun.

The mind, both empty and ever bright,
A canvas vast, a field of light.
The pulse of life, the song of air,
Just this moment, whole and bare.

Let go, breathe deep, release the strain,
Unfold in the vastness, free of pain.
For in this flow, this unbroken tide,
You are the ocean, the wave, the ride.

Commentary: "In the Midst of the Whirlwind"

This poem beautifully captures the essence of Dzogchen, inviting us to find liberation not by escaping our busy lives, but by recognizing the true nature of our minds within them. It echoes the profound insights passed down by a lineage of enlightened masters, from the early Indian figures to the great Tibetan tertöns and contemporary teachers who have kept the flame of Dzogchen alive. Let's break it down stanza by stanza.

Stanza 1: The Illusion of Striving

> In this age of flickering screens, Of shattered moments and restless dreams, We race on roads with no true end, Chasing reflections, forgetting to bend.

This opening vividly paints a picture of our contemporary existence. The *flickering screens* and *shattered moments* speak to the distractions and fragmentation of modern life. We are perpetually *racing* and *chasing reflections*, implying a constant outward search for fulfillment that is ultimately illusory. The phrase *forgetting to bend* suggests a loss of flexibility, adaptability, and perhaps, humility, in our relentless pursuit. This struggle against the unceasing pace of conditioned existence is precisely what Dzogchen seeks to transcend, as taught by masters like **Garab Dorje**, who emphasized the direct recognition of our true state.

> But here, in the quiet folds of time, A whisper rises, ancient, sublime— "You are already whole, already bright, A sun unclouded, a boundless light."

Here, the poem introduces the core Dzogchen insight. Amidst the chaos, a *whisper*—a subtle, profound truth—emerges. It's *ancient, sublime*, indicating its timeless and ultimate nature, a truth passed down from **Manjushrimitra** and **Shri Singha**. The whisper reveals that our true self is *already whole, already bright*, a direct counter to the fragmented self of the previous lines. The metaphors of *a sun unclouded* and *a boundless light* powerfully convey the inherent luminosity and unconditioned nature of **Rigpa**, untouched by any obscuration. This unclouded clarity is the very essence pointed to by **Padmasambhava** when he brought these teachings to Tibet.

> No need to mend, no need to chase, No fractured self to rearrange. Let go of striving, the ceaseless pace, And find the stillness, vast and strange.

This stanza offers the radical Dzogchen antidote to our restless striving. It emphasizes that our true nature doesn't need *mending* or *rearranging* because it's never been broken or out of order. The imperative to *let go of striving, the ceaseless pace* is central to Dzogchen, which is known as the effortless path. The poem promises that by releasing this effort, we can *find the stillness, vast and strange*—a profound, unconditioned awareness that might feel unfamiliar to the ego-driven mind. This non-striving is a key theme continually emphasized by my teacher.

Stanza 2: The Play of Awareness

> In the heartbeat of this rushing age, Let the mind unfurl, let the thoughts engage, Not as burdens, but as fleeting play, Waves in an ocean, a timeless sway.

Here, the poem explicitly brings the Dzogchen understanding of mind into the everyday *heartbeat of this rushing age.* Instead of fighting thoughts, we are encouraged to *let the mind unfurl* and *let the thoughts engage.* The key is the shift in perception: thoughts are *not as burdens, but as fleeting play.* This transforms our relationship with our inner experience. The beautiful metaphor of *waves in an ocean, a timeless sway* perfectly illustrates how individual thoughts and emotions arise and subside within the boundless, unchanging expanse of **Rigpa**, without disturbing its fundamental nature. This understanding of phenomena as the *play of awareness* is a hallmark of Dzogchen, articulated powerfully by masters such as **Longchen Rabjam.**

> Each breath, a bridge, a gentle trace, Each thought, a cloud in empty space. Let the dance of life be free, unplanned, Let the river flow, unheld, unspanned.

The poem offers practical anchors for this shift. *Each breath* becomes a conscious *bridge* to presence. *Each thought* is likened to *a cloud in empty space*, reiterating the impermanent and insubstantial nature of mental phenomena within the vastness of awareness (the *empty space*). The call to *let the dance of life be free, unplanned* and *let the river flow, unheld, unspanned* emphasizes the spontaneous, effortless, and unmanipulated nature of being that is intrinsic to Dzogchen.

For in this fleeting, fractured sphere, The open sky remains ever clear. No path to walk, no race to run, Just resting in the light of the primordial sun.

This stanza powerfully reaffirms the unchanging nature of **Rigpa** amidst impermanence. Despite the *fleeting, fractured sphere* of samsaric existence, the *open sky remains ever clear*—a strong metaphor for the **primordial purity (Ka-dag)** of the Ground. This understanding of innate purity is central to all Dzogchen traditions, including those of Bön, as taught by **Yongdzin Lopön Tenzin Namdak Rinpoche** and **His Holiness the 33rd Menri Trizin**. The lines *No path to walk, no race to run* underscore Dzogchen as the direct path, where there is nothing to achieve or strive for. The final image, *Just resting in the light of the primordial sun*, evokes the radiant, self-existing luminosity of **Rigpa**, our original, untainted nature, a truth emphasized by **Namkhai Norbu Rinpoche** in his teachings on natural freedom.

Stanza 3: The Unity of Being

> The mind, both empty and ever bright, A canvas vast,
> a field of light. The pulse of life, the song of air, Just
> this moment, whole and bare.

This stanza directly speaks to the inseparable unity of **emptiness and clarity** in **Rigpa**. The mind is *both empty and ever bright*, capturing its formless yet luminous quality. It's *A canvas vast*, signifying its empty potential for all appearances, and *a field of light*, highlighting its inherent radiance. The poem then grounds this abstract understanding in the immediate sensory experience: *The pulse of life, the song of air*, affirming that this ultimate reality is not separate from our ordinary experience. It's simply *Just this moment, whole and bare*—the unadorned, complete presence of now. This directness reflects the approach of masters like **Jigme Lingpa** and **Garchen Rinpoche**, who guide practitioners to the immediate, unmediated experience of Rigpa.

> Let go, breathe deep, release the strain, Unfold in the vastness, free of pain. For in this flow, this unbroken tide, You are the ocean, the wave, the ride.

The concluding lines offer a final, compassionate instruction: *Let go, breathe deep, release the strain.* This simple yet profound practice allows us to *unfold in the vastness, free of pain*, as suffering arises from resistance and clinging, not from the nature of phenomena themselves. The poem culminates with a powerful metaphor for non-duality: *You are the ocean, the wave, the ride.* This encapsulates the Dzogchen view that the individual (the wave) is never separate from the ultimate reality (the ocean), and the entire experience of life (the ride) is simply the spontaneous manifestation of this indivisible unity. There is no separation between the experiencer, the experience, and the fundamental ground of being. This ultimate unity, where all distinctions dissolve into the boundless expanse, is the profound insight offered by the entire lineage of Dzogchen.

Primordial Purity (Ka-dag)

ཀ་དག་སྣང་བའི་རྒྱ་འབར་པ།
མི་འོང་མི་འགག་འདུས་མ་བྱུང་།
ཡིད་ཀྱི་རྣམ་སྣང་སྣང་བར་ཐོད།
གང་ཡང་མེད་པར་འགྲོ་བའི་དབྱིངས།

Spontaneous Presence (Lhun-drub)

ལྷུན་གྲུབ་རང་རྒྱན་གྱི་འོད་དཔག་པ།
འདུས་མ་བྱས་གང་ཡང་མེད་པ།
རང་རིག་ཡེ་ཤེས་སྣང་བའི་དབྱིངས།
རང་གྲུར་རིག་པ་གང་ཡང་མེད་པ།

Unity of Emptiness and Clarity (Od-sal Song-yug)

སྣང་སྟོང་མཉམ་པར་བྱེད་པའི་རྣམ་དབྱིངས།
སྟོང་པ་ལ་སྣང་བར་སྣང་བར་བབས།
སྣང་བ་འོད་ཀྱི་སྙིང་པོ་རང་འབྱུང་།
གང་ཡང་མེད་པའི་རིག་པའི་དབྱིངས།

Self-Arising Wisdom (Rang-byung Yeshe)

རང་འབྱུང་ཡེ་ཤེས་རང་འབྱུང་གི་སྣང་།
གང་ཡང་མེད་པར་གང་ཡང་སྤྱོད།
རིག་པའི་སྣང་བ་རང་གྲུར་སྣང་བ།
དཀར་པོའི་རང་གྲུར་ལུང་འགྲོའི་རྒྱལ།

The Ground (Gzhi)

གཞི་མི་འོང་མི་འགག་གང་ཡང་མེད་པ།
གཉིས་མེད་ཡེ་ཤེས་གཞི་གང་ཡང་མེད།
སྟོང་པའི་མཐའ་མེད་གཞི་རང་འབྱུང་།
རིག་པའི་སྣང་བ་གཉིས་མེད་འབྱུང་།

Nature of Mind (Sem-nyid)

འོད་གསལ་རང་གྱུར་སེམས་གཞན་མེད་པ།
གཞི་གྱི་མི་འོང་མི་འགག་གང་ཡང་མེད།
རང་གྱུར་རིག་པའི་འོད་གསལ་འགྲོའི་གནས།
སེམས་ཀྱི་སྣང་བ་འགྲོ་བའི་རྣལ་དབང་།

Effortless Being

མི་ཙུང་དགེ་བའི་རང་རིག་དང་སྦྱོད།
མི་སྦྱུད་རང་གྱུར་འདུས་མ་བྱུས།
རང་གྱུར་སྣང་བའི་རིག་པ་མི་སྦྱུད་པ།
འགྲོ་བའི་རང་རིག་གང་ཡང་མེད་པ།

Self-Liberation (Rang-grol)

རང་གྱུར་རིག་པ་འབྱུང་བ་སྐྱེད་པ་མེད།
རང་འབྱུང་གྲོགས་པའི་རིག་པ་རང་གྱུར།
གང་ཡང་མེད་པའི་འོད་གསལ་རང་འབྱུང་།
གཉིས་མེད་གཞི་རང་གྱུར་རིག་པ།

Primordial Purity (Ka-dag)
In the silence before the first breath,
where sky is pure and winds are unborn,
know yourself as the clear, unblemished vastness,
the endless, stainless ground of all.

Spontaneous Presence (Lhun-drub)
Like a river that sings without source,
or a flame that dances without cause,
rest in the radiant pulse of this moment,
where being and becoming kiss.

Unity of Emptiness and Clarity (Od-sal Song-yug)
Empty, yet the moon reflects,
clear, yet the void remains,
see the dance of light and space,
inseparable, ever one.

Self-Arising Wisdom (Rang-byung Yeshe)
From the heart of boundless knowing,
arises the song of all that is,
not grasped nor lost, yet ever known,
the birthless, deathless breath of truth.

The Ground (Gzhi)
The mirror knows no dust,
the sky, no weight of passing clouds,
be the depthless ground of all,
where forms arise and fall like dreams.

Nature of Mind (Sem-nyid)
Before the wave, before the thought,
a knowing clear as mountain air,
beyond all reach, beyond all grasp,
the mind's true face, forever bare.

Effortless Being
Sit as the mountain, breathe as the wind,
move as the river, clear and free,
no path, no goal, just this –
the easy flow of what is.

Self-Liberation (Rang-grol)
Thoughts arise like morning mist,
fade like echoes in a canyon,
see their empty, radiant dance,
and they dissolve without a trace.

Dzogchen in Verse: The Heart of Natural Perfection

This poem distills the profound essence of Dzogchen, offering a lyrical journey through its core principles. Each stanza, followed by commentary, illuminates a facet of our primordial nature, echoing the wisdom of a vast lineage of enlightened masters.

Primordial Purity (*Ka-dag*)

> *In the silence before the first breath, where sky is pure and winds are unborn, know yourself as the clear, unblemished vastness, the endless, stainless ground of all.*

Commentary: This stanza evokes **Ka-dag** (*ka dag*), the **primordial purity** that is the **essence of mind**—utterly stainless, beyond birth and death. As **Longchenpa** teaches, this purity is not merely the absence of defilement, but the original, unconditioned ground that is always present. **Garab Dorje's** direct introduction points to this: recognition is effortless because this purity is already your nature. Masters like **Yongdzin Tenzin Namdak** and **Shardza Tashi Gyaltsen** emphasize that Ka-dag transcends all dualities and conceptual elaborations; it is the *sky before clouds*, untouched by any arising phenomena.

Spontaneous Presence (*Lhun-drub*)

> *Like a river that sings without source, or a flame that dances without cause, rest in the radiant pulse of this moment, where being and becoming kiss.*

Commentary: Lhun-drub (*lhun grub*) is the **spontaneous, self-arising display** of wisdom and phenomena. It is the dynamic aspect of the Ground—manifesting effortlessly, without cause or fabrication. **Vimalamitra** and **Manjushrimitra** taught that this presence is not created by practice; it unfolds naturally when resting in Ka-dag. **Tenzin Wangyal Rinpoche** and **Tempa Dukte Lama** describe it as the *natural radiance* of awareness, the effortless play of wisdom in every moment. It's the inherent luminosity that emanates from the empty ground, like **sunlight radiating from the sun**, needing no external source or effort to shine.

Unity of Emptiness and Clarity (*Od-sal Stong-yug*)

> *Empty, yet the moon reflects, clear, yet the void remains, see the dance of light and space, inseparable, ever one.*

Commentary: This unity is the heart of Dzogchen and Mahamudra: **emptiness** (*stong pa*) and **clarity** (*'od gsal*) are not separate. **Padmasambhava** and **Yeshe Tsogyal** taught that all appearances are the **play of luminous emptiness**—like **reflections in a mirror**. The mirror itself is empty of the images, yet its clarity allows them to appear. **Longchenpa** describes this inseparability as the *natural state*, where light and space, knowing and void, are a single taste. It is this indivisible quality of **Rigpa**

that allows for the arising of all phenomena without compromising its pristine nature.

Self-Arising Wisdom (*Rang-byung Yeshe*)

> From the heart of boundless knowing, arises the song of all that is, not grasped nor lost, yet ever known, the birthless, deathless breath of truth.

Commentary: Rang-byung Yeshe (*rang byung ye shes*) is the **wisdom that arises spontaneously** from the Ground. It is not acquired, but revealed when the mind rests in its own nature. Masters like **Shri Singha** and **Jnanasutra** stress that this wisdom is self-arising—beyond effort, beyond seeking. It is the *song of all that is*, echoing the teachings of **Namkhai Norbu Rinpoche** and **Tulku Urgyen Rinpoche**, who remind us that realization is simply the recognition of what has always been—the inherent knowing that is never diminished or enhanced.

The Ground (*Gzhi*)

> *The mirror knows no dust, the sky, no weight of passing clouds, be the depthless ground of all, where forms arise and fall like dreams.*

Commentary: The **Ground** (*gzhi*) is the **base of all experience**—empty, pure, and unchanging. It is the **mirror that reflects all phenomena without being affected**, and the **sky that witnesses passing clouds without alteration**. Masters like

Menri Lopon Rinpoche and **Latri Nyima Dakpa Rinpoche** in the Bön tradition, and **Dodrupchen Rinpoche** in the Nyingma, teach that recognizing the Ground is recognizing the unshakeable foundation of reality, where nothing is ever truly gained or lost, as all arises and falls within its boundless expanse, like **dreams within the consciousness of the dreamer**.

Nature of Mind (*Sem-nyid*)

> *Before the wave, before the thought, a knowing clear as mountain air, beyond all reach, beyond all grasp, the mind's true face, forever bare.*

Commentary: Sem-nyid (*sems nyid*) is the very **nature of mind**—luminous, empty, and self-knowing. It is not an object to be found, but the subjectivity that is always present, prior to any conceptualization or dualistic perception. **Jigme Lingpa** and **Jamgon Kongtrul Lodrö Thaye** describe it as *clear as mountain air*, untouched by conceptual elaboration. **Khandro Rinpoche** and **Pema Khandro Rinpoche** emphasize that this recognition is the heart of all practice, a direct apprehension of our intrinsic purity that exists *before the wave* of thought or emotion arises.

Effortless Being

> Sit as the mountain, breathe as the wind, move as the river, clear and free, no path, no goal, just this – the easy flow of what is.

Commentary: Effortlessness is the hallmark of Dzogchen. As **Nyoshul Khenpo Rinpoche** and **Mingyur Rinpoche** teach, the natural state is revealed not by striving, but by relaxing completely. The *mountain, wind, and river* are classic metaphors for stability, breath, and flow—reminding us that our true nature is found in effortless presence. It's about letting go of all fabrication and manipulation, allowing the **spontaneous presence of Lhun-drub** to unfold naturally, like the **unhindered course of a stream**.

Self-Liberation (*Rang-grol*)

> *Thoughts arise like morning mist, fade like echoes in a canyon, see their empty, radiant dance, and they dissolve without a trace.*

Commentary: Self-liberation (*rang grol*) is the recognition that thoughts and emotions, when seen in their true nature, liberate themselves. As **Garab Dorje** and **Vairotsana** taught, there is nothing to reject or transform—just see clearly, and all dissolves. They are like **morning mist** or **echoes in a canyon**—they appear vividly but lack true substance and vanish without effort. **Sogyal Rinpoche** and **Chökyi Nyima Rinpoche** echo this: liberation is not an act, but a natural process when awareness is unobstructed, recognizing the inherent **empty, radiant dance** of phenomena.

The Uncontrived Path

All the great masters—ancient and modern, Bön and Nyingma—agree:

- The natural state is **primordially pure (*Ka-dag*)**, **spontaneously present (*Lhun-drub*)**, and **inseparable from wisdom and compassion.**
- **Recognition is effortless**: it is a matter of relaxing, resting, and allowing the mind to reveal its own face. It's not about adding something, but about uncovering what's already there, like **revealing a statue by removing its clay mold.**
- **Self-liberation is not a goal to reach**, but the natural unfolding of awareness when left uncontrived, akin to **clouds naturally dispersing in the sky**.

As **Keith Dowman** writes, *"Dzogchen is the pathless path: nothing to do, nowhere to go, just this—now, as it is."* The teachings of **Tenzin Wangyal Rinpoche**, **Tempa Dukte Lama**, and all the listed masters continually point us back to this:

Rest in the natural state; recognize your own face; let all phenomena arise and dissolve in the vastness of your true being, which is the **all-pervasive, unwavering Ground**. This is the ultimate freedom, found not by seeking, but by simply being.

Primordial Purity

(Ka-dag, ཀ་དག་)

Ka-dag is consistently described as the ever-present, unchanging purity of mind, realized through direct, effortless recognition—not through effort or conceptual analysis, but by resting in the natural state

- **Ka-dag is not merely the absence of impurity**—it **transcends the dichotomy of pure and impure.**
- The term **Ka-dag** (ཀ་དག་) is often translated as **"original purity" or "alpha purity,"** underscoring the **self-existing clarity of mind.**
- **Recognition of Ka-dag** is the **key to liberation**—rather than striving to purify the mind, the practitioner **rests in the natural state**, allowing **self-arising** wisdom to manifest effortlessly.

Ka-dag refers to the primordial purity of Rigpa—its intrinsic, untainted nature. Unlike conventional spiritual paths that emphasize gradual purification, Dzogchen asserts that Rigpa is already pure and simply needs to be recognized rather than attained.

In the traditions of **Dzogchen** and **Mahamudra**, the highest realization is not achieved through struggle or gradual purification, but through the **effortless recognition** of **rigpa**—the **primordial, luminous awareness** that is our **true nature**. This recognition does not require constructing or fabricating a new state; rather, it is a **direct introduction** to what has always been present but is habitually overlooked.

To awaken to this reality is to **shift from seeking to seeing**, from striving to simply **being**. The journey unfolds not as a process of transformation, but as **the revelation of what has never been absent**.

Philosophical Insights

-

Trekchö (*khregs chod*): This practice focuses on **"cutting through"** or directly recognizing the primordial purity (**Ka-dag**) of the mind's essence. It's about settling into the unconditioned ground, resting in the naked awareness that is free from all thoughts and concepts. This is like **becoming the vast, clear sky**. It's the foundational stability from which Tögal can then naturally unfold. This "cutting through" is a direct lineage from masters like **Vairotsana**.

Ka-dag and the Ground (Gzhi, གཞི་)

- Ka-dag is closely related to the Essence aspect of the Ground (Gzhi).
- The Ground is characterized by emptiness—it lacks inherent existence and is primordially pure.
- Ka-dag transcends all mental constructs, representing the natural, unchanging purity of the base.

Spontaneous Presence

(Lhun-drub, ལྷུན་གྲུབ་)

Definition and Significance

Lhun-drub refers to the **self-arising, spontaneous manifestation of Rigpa**. It is the **dynamic expression of primordial purity**, where **wisdom unfolds effortlessly**.

Key Teachings on Lhun-drub

- Lhun-drub is the **natural radiance of Rigpa**, beyond effort or contrivance.
- **Padmasambhava:** Emphasizes that **spontaneous presence is the natural display of awakened awareness**.

Philosophical Insights

- **Lhun-drub is the dynamic aspect of Rigpa**—it is not separate from Ka-dag but its natural expression.
- Wisdom manifests spontaneously when the mind is free from grasping and effort.
- Recognition of Lhun-drub leads to **effortless realization**, where **awareness and manifestation are inseparable**.

The Heart Essence of Dzogchen

Dzogchen, the Great Perfection, is not a path of becoming, nor of effort, progression, or purification. It is the direct, naked recognition of what *is*—our own awareness, timelessly free and unconstructed. In the words of Garab Dorje, the original transmitter of Dzogchen to human beings: **"Direct introduction to one's own nature—recognize what has always been."**

Within the vast sky of Dzogchen teachings, two methods form the wings of realization: **Trekchö** and **Tögal**. They are not sequential stages, but complementary gateways to the same vast expanse—the inseparable unity of primordial purity (*Ka-dag*) and spontaneous presence (*Lhun-drub*).

Trekchö (ཁྲེགས་ཆོད་)

Cutting Through to Primordial Purity

Trekchö means "cutting through"—cutting through grasping, illusion, mental fabrication, and effort. It is the fearless plunge into the ever-present, stainless nature of mind. This nature is not something to be improved or acquired; it is uncovered through direct recognition and effortless abiding.

> **Yongdzin Lopön Tenzin Namdak Rinpoche**:
> *"The natural state is not something to be created; it is always present. Trekchö is simply to recognize and remain in that state."*

In the practice of Trekchö, all appearances, sensations, and thoughts are allowed to arise and dissolve like waves in the ocean. One does not follow them nor push them away. Rather, one rests in the *View*—the recognition that all phenomena are mere reflections in the mirror-like expanse of awareness.

> **Shardza Tashi Gyaltsen**:
> *"Rest in the nature of mind, free from effort; let appearances come and go, like reflections in a mirror."*

There is no need to alter the mind, improve it, or force concentration. As **Padmasambhava** teaches:
"Rest in the natural state, free from contrivance; appearances and emptiness are inseparable."

The essence of Trekchö is simplicity:

- **Sit quietly**, letting the breath be natural.
- **Do not grasp or reject** any experience.
- **Recognize awareness itself**—spacious, luminous, and unchanging.

Trekchö reveals the sky-like nature of mind—vast, open, and free from cloud-like obscurations.

Integration of Ka-dag and Lhun-drub

The Unity of Primordial Purity and Spontaneous Presence

- Ka-dag is the essence—the primordial purity of mind.
- Lhun-drub is the manifestation—the spontaneous unfolding of wisdom.
- Realizing their unity is the culmination of the Dzogchen path.

Practical Integration in Everyday Life

- Rest in awareness without effort—recognizing that Rigpa is already present.
- Allow thoughts and emotions to self-liberate—like clouds dissolving in the sky.
- Engage with reality without grasping—seeing all phenomena as the spontaneous display of Rigpa.

The first step is to discover pure being. To trust, prioritize above all things liberation, then the path is abide. Let go, breath. The great **Dzogchen non-dual tradition** presents **Rigpa as the direct recognition of the ultimate ground of existence**. Through **Ka-dag (Primordial Purity)** and Lhun-drub (Spontaneous Presence), practitioners awaken to their true nature, beyond conceptual obscurations and dualistic perception

རང་བཞིན་གྱི་ངོ་བོས།

བསམ་གཏན་དང་དུས་ལས་འདས་པའི་ངང་ལ།
ཉི་མའི་འགྲོད་དང་བཞག་པའི་ཞི་བ་མེད།
རྒྱ་མེད་ཀྱི་རིག་པ་གསལ་བ་དག།
རང་བཞིན་གྱི་ཡེ་ཤེས་ཤིན་ཏུ་ཡང་དག། །

'འཇིག་རྟེན་གྱི་ཐམས་ཅད་གཅིག་ཏུ་འདུས།
འཆིང་བ་དང་འདོད་ཆགས་ལགས་མེད་པས།
འཇིགས་པ་དང་འཛོལ་བ་ཐམས་ཅད་སྤྱངས།
མ་ཆགས་མ་འཛིན་གྱི་མི་འགྲུགས་པ། །

རང་བཞིན་དང་ལྡན་པའི་དབྱིངས་སུ་གནས།
བརྩོད་པ་མེད་པ་རང་ཆས་སུ་བཞག།
སྔ་མ་དང་ཕྱི་མའི་རྣམ་རྟོག་ལ།
སེམས་མི་འཛིན་པར་དེང་སངས་ལ་བཞག། །

ནང་གི་ནམ་མཁའ་དང་ཕྱི་རོལ་རྒྱ་མཚོ།
ཐམས་ཅད་རང་ལས་རང་ཤར་གྱི་ངོ་བོ་ཉིད། །

In the Pure Self

In the stillness beyond thought and time,
A silent warmth, serene, sublime.
Mind's depths settle in natural ease,
Clarity shines with effortless peace.

In self-luminous awareness, free and wide,
All things as one are unified.
Let go of fear, release desire—
The fire of grasping, now expired.

In harmony with nature's flow,
No need to strive, just let it go.
Past and future—phantoms fade,
Rest now, unafraid.

Inner sky and outer vast,
One unfolding field, boundless and vast.

རང་བཞིན་གྱི་ངོ་བོས། — "In the Nature of the Self"

This refers to the *primordial essence* of one's being — the ultimate nature (*rang bzhin*) of mind, which in Dzogchen is known as *rigpa* (pure awareness), untouched by dualistic thought.

Verse 1: Resting in Natural Awareness

བསམ་གཏན་དང་དུས་ལས་འདས་པའི་ངང་ལ།
In the state beyond thought and time,
This describes resting in a meditative state (*ngang*), free from conceptual elaboration and beyond the flow of linear time.

ཉི་མའི་འགྲོད་དང་བཞག་པའི་ཞི་བ་མེད།
A warmth like sunlight, settled, brings peace.
A poetic metaphor for the innate warmth and stillness of resting in awareness. "Sunlight" represents clarity and calm.

རྒྱུ་མེད་ཀྱི་རིག་པ་གསལ་བ་དག།
The unfabricated awareness shines clear and pure.
Rigpa (awareness) is described as "causeless" (*rgyu med*), meaning it is not created — it is ever-present and self-arising.

རང་བཞིན་གྱི་ཡེ་ཤེས་ཤིན་ཏུ་ཡང་དག།
Primordial wisdom, the natural state, is utterly pure.

Ye shes (primordial wisdom) is spontaneous and unaltered — the direct realization of one's own mind's nature.

Verse 2: Letting Go of Clinging

འཛིག་རྟེན་གྱི་ཐམས་ཅད་གཅིག་ཏུ་འདུས།
All phenomena of the world are unified as one.
A Dzogchen view: appearances are not separate — they all arise within the expanse of awareness.

འཆིང་བ་དང་འདོད་ཆགས་ལགས་མེད་པས།
There is no bondage, no desire to bind us.
True freedom is the absence of attachment and aversion — nothing can ensnare the natural mind.

འཛིགས་པ་དང་འཛོལ་བ་ཐམས་ཅད་སྤངས།
Fears and regrets are completely let go.
Fear arises from dualistic fixation; when resting in *rigpa*, these fall away.

མ་ཆགས་མ་འཛིན་གྱི་མེ་འཕྲུགས་པ།
The fire of clinging is extinguished in non-attachment.
This line echoes Dzogchen's pointing out of the mind's tendency to grasp. Here, clinging burns out in the cool space of letting go.

Verse 3: Natural Harmony and the Present

རང་བཞིན་དང་ལྡན་པའི་དབྱིངས་སུ་གནས།
Abiding in the space infused with naturalness,
Dbyings (space/expanse) here refers to the all-encompassing presence of awareness. No need to fabricate or adjust anything.

བརྩོད་པ་མེད་པ་རང་ཆས་སུ་བཞག།

Free from struggle, one rests as one truly is.
There is no striving, no conflict — one simply abides in *rang chas* (one's own nature).

སྔ་མ་དང་ཕྱི་མའི་རྣམ་རྟོག་ལ།

Thoughts of past and future,
Past and future are just mental projections (*rnam rtog*) — not reality.

སེམས་མི་འཛིན་པར་དེང་སངས་ལ་བཞག།

Are not grasped—rest now, awake and present.
The key Dzogchen instruction: *do not grasp* (mi 'dzin) thoughts. Just *rest in awareness* in the present moment.

Verse 4: Unity of Inner and Outer Reality

ནང་གི་ནམ་མཁའ་དང་ཕྱི་རོལ་རྒྱ་མཚོ།

The inner sky and the outer ocean,
Sky symbolizes openness and clarity of mind; ocean symbolizes the vastness of phenomena.

ཐམས་ཅད་རང་ལས་རང་ཤར་གྱི་ངོ་བོ་ཉིད།

All arise self-originated, as the nature of being itself.
Everything emerges spontaneously from the *rang shes* — the self-knowing nature of awareness.

This poem expresses core **Dzogchen principles**:

- Resting in *rigpa*, the uncontrived awareness
- Letting go of attachment and fear

- Living in harmony with nature and the present
- Realizing that everything arises from one's own innate awareness

In ancient times, debates arose between Buddhist monks and Hindus about Shamatha, arguing that it would not liberate you from suffering but is merely a placebo. They contended that one must meditate on emptiness, or limitless space. This perspective is true from the Sutra viewpoint, but in Dzogchen, it is the inseparable and spontaneous union of space and clear light.

When the mind becomes scattered or bored, make a small effort. Relax slightly if too tense or agitated. Eventually, dependence on external objects will diminish, allowing the practitioner to meditate without an object.

"Do not dwell in the past, do not dream of the future, concentrate the mind on the present moment." — Buddha

No matter the philosophical system or culture, at the end we arrive at the same place to be, just to be, expand the mind, if we abide, we glow in bliss.

Taoist meditation, much like Buddhist meditation, emphasizes stillness and inner peace.However, it also includes practices designed to harmonize the body's energy flow, known as **Qi**. Techniques such as **Zhan Zhuang** (standing meditation) and **Nei Dan** (inner alchemy) aim to balance the mind, body, and spirit, aligning with the Taoist principle of living in harmony with the Tao, the fundamental nature of the universe.

Lao Tzu, the founder of Taoism, expressed this eloquently: "To the mind that is still, the whole universe surrenders."

Buddhist meditation often aims at liberation from Samsara and attaining Enlightenment, while Taoist meditation seeks harmony with the Tao and balancing the body's energies. While both traditions use breath-focused and mindfulness practices.

- **Stillness and Tranquility:** Ancient traditions advocate for calming the mind and achieving a state of inner peace.

- **Natural Awareness:** Recognizing the natural state of the mind and the fundamental interconnectedness of all things.

- **Non-Attachment:** Letting go of desires, fears, thoughts and attachments to achieve spiritual freedom.

- **Harmony with Nature:** Emphasizing the importance of living in harmony with the natural world.

"In dwelling, live close to the ground. In thinking, keep to the simple. In conflict, be fair and generous. In governing, don't try to control. At work, do what you enjoy. In family life, be completely present." — Lao Tzu

No matter the philosophical system or culture, at the end we arrive at the same place to be, just to be, expand the mind, if we abide, we glow in bliss.

1. Resting in Awareness During Challenges

- **If we abide in awareness at all times breath deeply, in this spacious experience, we are flexible like water. For instance if we are delayed during travel,** instead of **reacting with frustration,** one **pauses to observe bodily sensations and thoughts,** allowing **calm and clarity to arise.**

2. Transforming Daily Activities into Meditation

- **Simple acts like walking in nature or washing dishes** become **opportunities for deep awareness.**
- **Recognizing Rigpa during ordinary experiences dissolves the boundary between spiritual practice and daily life.**

བསྡུས་དོན། — Summary Table

Aspect	Description
Dzogchen & Non-Dual Traditions	Shares **direct realization focus** with Advaita Vedanta & Zen, but uniquely **emphasizes emptiness and self-liberation.**
Rigpa's Core Nature	Reflexively **self-aware wisdom**—primordial **purity and luminosity.**
Mind as a Mirror	Thoughts **arise & dissolve without altering awareness**—encourages **non-clinging.**
Spontaneous Liberation	**Rang-grol**—thoughts & emotions **self-liberate when not grasped.**
Integration into Life	Daily activities **become practice**, allowing **continuous presence.**

བརྗེད་ཏེ་སྨོལ་བ། — Conclusion

Dzogchen provides a **living path** that **seamlessly integrates spiritual realization** into **modern existence.** By **resting effortlessly in Rigpa**, practitioners **dissolve dualistic patterns, embody wisdom and compassion**, and **awaken to the ever-present luminous expanse of awareness.**

ཚོར་བ་དང་རིག་པ། — Navigating Emotions with Wisdom in Dzogchen

The Dzogchen view says to us to **"Let emotions arise and dissolve—like waves, never separate from the ocean."** This profound insight encourages us to **observe our emotional landscape with non-judgmental awareness**, recognizing that emotions are **transient expressions of our fundamental nature**, much like **waves arising and subsiding in the vast ocean of awareness.**

རིག་པའི་རྩད་དང་ཚོར་བ་རང་བྱུང་། — The Self-Liberation of Emotions

- **Emotions are not obstacles** but **natural manifestations of awareness.**
- **Neither indulging in nor rejecting emotions** allows them to **self-liberate.**
- **Recognizing their empty nature** prevents them from **solidifying into suffering.**
- **Resting in awareness** rather than **identifying with emotions** dissolves their grip.

Example: Applying Dzogchen to Emotional Turmoil

Imagine feeling overwhelmed by frustration. Instead of suppressing or fueling it, **pause and observe**:

- **Where does this frustration arise?**
- **Does it have substance, or does it dissolve when observed?**
- **Can I rest in the awareness that perceives it, rather than being consumed by it?**

By **resting in Rigpa**, frustration **loses its solidity**, revealing **the spacious clarity beneath.**

དམ་ཚིག་དང་རིག་པ་རང་བྱུང་། — Acting from Clarity, Not Effort

Dzogchen guides us to **"Act from clarity—not from effort, but from deep presence."** This embodies the principle of **"doing by not doing"**, where actions **arise spontaneously** from **profound presence and awareness**, rather than being **driven by striving, attachment, or conceptual planning**.

Example: Effortless Action in Daily Life

- **A musician deeply immersed in playing does not "try" to create music—it flows naturally.**
- **A compassionate response to someone's suffering arises effortlessly when connected to awareness.**
- **Decisions made from clarity feel intuitive, rather than forced or anxious.**

When **deeply connected to intrinsic awareness**, actions become **a natural expression of wisdom and compassion**, flowing **effortlessly in response to the needs of the moment**.

རིག་པའི་གཞུང་དང་སྨོན་འགྲོ། — The Essence of Freedom in Dzogchen

The **essence of freedom** in Dzogchen lies in the **simple yet profound practice** of:

1. **Resting in the natural state of mind.**
2. **Directly recognizing our innate Buddha nature (Rigpa, རིག་པ).**
3. **Simply being present in that recognition.**

This state of **resting, recognizing, and being** is the **ultimate freedom**, the **"fantastic flow of true nature, the completion already present."**

བསྡུས་དོན། — Summary Table

Aspect	Description	Example
Navigating Emotions	**Observing emotions as transient waves,** allowing **self-liberation.**	**Pausing when frustrated, resting in awareness rather than reacting.**
Acting from Clarity	**Actions arise spontaneously from deep presence**, not effort.	**A musician immersed in playing, a compassionate response flowing naturally.**
Essence of Freedom	**Resting, recognizing, and simply being in Rigpa.**	**Letting go of striving, resting in the natural state.**

རྫོགས་ཆེན་གཞུང་དང་སྦྱོན་འགྲོ། — Conclusion

Integrating Dzogchen principles into modern life offers **a timeless path to inner peace and freedom.** By **understanding and applying the core tenets** of:

- **Direct recognition,**
- **Spontaneous liberation,**
- **Inherent compassion,**
- **Effortless being,**
- **Present-moment awareness,**

Individuals can **transform their relationship with themselves and the world.**

This **journey of awakening**, characterized by **resting, recognizing, and simply being**, holds the **potential to transform mental samsara into the very dance of awakening in our everyday lives.**

རང་གནས་ལ་འཚོར།
དབྱིངས་དང་གཞི། འབར་བའི་རང་བྱུང་གཟུགས།
མི་འགྲོ་མི་ལྡོག་མི་འགྱུར།
རང་གནས་གང་ཅུང་། ལྷུན་གྲུབ་སྟོང་པའི་དགའ་སྟོན།
གཉིས་མེད་དང་། མེད་པའི་གཉིས།
གཅིག་པའི་དབྱིངས་ཀྱི་བརྗོད་མེད།

གནས་ནས་འབར། རང་གནས་ནང་འབར།
འཁྲུལ་མེད་འདོད་མེད་འཁོར་མེད།
དབྱིངས་དང་སྦྲ། དངོས་པོ་དང་སྦྲ།
ལྷུན་གྲུབ་དབྱིངས་ལ་རྟོགས།
མི་དབང་མི་གནས། རང་བྱུང་རང་གནས།
རང་གནས་ནས་འབར། གནས་ནས་འབར།

རང་གནས་འགྲོ་མེད་བརྡུད་པ་མེད།
བརྡུད་པ་མེད་འགྲོ་མེད།
རང་གནས་འཁྲུལ་མེད་རང་གནས།
བསམ་བློ་འབར། གཏིང་དུ་འབར།
དབྱིངས་འཁོར་མེད་འདུག་དང་འབར།

འགྲོ་མེད། སྤྱོད་མེད། རང་འགྲུབ།
དབྱིངས་སྦྲིལ་མེད་འདུག་དང་འབར།
མི་འབར་མི་མངའ་མི་འཁོར།
འཁྲུལ་མེད་སྤྱོད་མེད་སྦྲ།
རང་གནས་ནས་འབར། རང་གནས་འབར།

དབྱིངས་གནས་མེད། དབྱིངས་འཁོར་མེད།
རང་གནས་སྦྲིལ་མེད་འབར།
མི་སྦྲིལ་མི་འབར། རང་གནས་ནས་འབར།

འགྲོ་མེད་རང་གནས་འཁོར་མེད།
དབྱིངས་ནས་འབར། འཁོར་ལས་འབར།
རང་བྱུང་དབྱིངས་གནས་འཁོར་མེད།
མེད་དང་མངའ། མི་དབང་མི་གནས།
རང་བྱུང་རང་གནས་ནས་འབར།

Self-Arising Compassion

Resting in the groundless ground,
The open sky of being, vast and sound.
No coming, no going, no trace, no mark,
Only the radiance of the boundless heart.

Effortless presence, pure and bright,
Spontaneous like morning light,
Unforced, unbound, no need to strive,
Just this awareness, fully alive.

No fixing, no mending, no need to change,
The luminous mind, free and strange.
Beyond the grasp of thought and name,
A ceaseless flow, a wordless flame.

The dance of form, the play of light,
The empty sky, the endless night,
No path to walk, no goal to gain,
Only the echo of the vast terrain.

Compassion, not a task to bear,
But the pulse of life, the open air,
A natural glow, a radiant field,
The heart's true warmth, forever revealed.

No burden to carry, no race to run,
The sky itself, the burning sun.
From this vastness, all forms arise,
Without effort, without disguise.

Just resting here, no coming, no going,
Like a river in its endless flowing.
The mind itself, the groundless ground,
Pure compassion, profoundly found.

ཐུགས་རྗེ་དང་རིག་པ། — Compassion and Rigpa in Dzogchen

Compassion (**Thugs rje, ཐུགས་རྗེ་**) in Dzogchen **transcends conventional notions** of emotion or ethical principle. It is **recognized as the very energy and responsiveness of Rigpa**, the **intrinsic dynamism of primordial awareness.**

རིག་པའི་རྣམ་དང་ཐུགས་རྗེ་རང་བྱུང་། — The Radiance of Universal Compassion

- **Compassion is not cultivated through effort** but **arises spontaneously** from the **direct realization of non-dual reality.**
- The **artificial separation between self and others dissolves**, revealing **the natural unfolding of wisdom.**
- **Compassion is inseparable from Rigpa**, representing the **pure awareness responding to the suffering and needs of all beings.**
- It serves as the **basis for enlightened activity**, such as the **emanation of Nirmanakayas (physical forms of Buddhas) to benefit sentient beings.**

Integrating Dzogchen Wisdom into Modern Life

1. Letting Go of Conceptual Clutter

- In modern life, we are **overwhelmed by information and expectations**, leading to **mental busyness** that **obscures innate clarity**.
- Dzogchen offers a **path to navigate this** by **detaching from limiting beliefs and habitual thought patterns.**
- **Recognizing thoughts as transient occurrences**, like **clouds drifting across the sky**, without **becoming entangled in their content.**

2. Observing Mental Events with Detached Awareness

- The **core practice** is to **observe thoughts and emotions** with **detached yet present awareness**, understanding their **fundamental emptiness.**
- **Cultivating present-moment awareness** involves **choosing to pause instead of striving**, allowing **inherent awareness to reveal itself naturally.**

3. Practicing Non-Judgmental Awareness

- Dzogchen encourages: > *"Observe without judgment—thoughts are clouds, you are the sky."*
- This fosters **a detached yet present awareness** of **inner and outer experiences.**
- **Simple mindfulness practices**, such as **focusing on the breath or bodily sensations**, serve as **accessible entry points** to cultivate **present-moment awareness.**

0རྫོགས་ཆེན་གཞུང་དང་སྒྲོན་འགྲོ།

By **resting effortlessly in Rigpa**, practitioners **dissolve dualistic patterns, embody wisdom and compassion**, and **awaken to the ever-present luminous expanse of awareness.**

Would you like **more refined techniques for practical integration**, or **insights into Dzogchen meditation methods**? There's **so much depth to explore** that goes **beyond intellectual understanding—it must be lived and embodied**!

རྒྱ་མཚོའི་འཁོར་ལོ།

དབྱིངས་ཀྱི་ནང་ལ་གནས་པར་བྱ།
འཁོར་ལོ་འཁོར་བར་འགྱུར་གྱིས་འབར།
གང་ཅང་གཏིང་དུ་འཁོར་རྒྱུན་ལྷ།
འཁོར་བའི་རླུང་། སྒྲུབ་མེད་པའི་རླུང་།

ཁོངས་འཛིན་མེད་པར་དབུས་ལ་གནས།
གཏིང་དུ་འཁོར་མེད་པའི་རྒྱ་མཚོ།
ཕྱོགས་མེད་པར་གནས་པའི་དབྱིངས།
འཁོར་འཁོར་མེད་པའི་མཐའ་མེད་རྒྱལ།

རྟོགས་པའི་སྣར་བཞིན་གཞི་གང་ཅང་།
འཁྲུལ་མེད་འགྲོ་མེད་པའི་འཁོར་ལོ།
འཁོར་ལོ་རླུང་དང་ལྷུག་པའི་འཁོར།
འགྲོ་མེད་པར་གནས་པའི་རྒྱ་མཚོ།

དབྱིངས་གཞི་འཁྲུལ་མེད་པའི་སྤྱོད།
འབྲལ་མེད་སྨུན་འོད་གཞན་མེད།

འཁོར་ལོ་མེད་པར་དབྱིངས་འཁྱིལ།
འཁོར་མེད་པའི་རྒྱ་མཚོའི་དབྱིངས།

རང་བྱུང་གཞི་འཁྲུལ་མེད་འགྲོ་མེད།
འཁོར་འཁོར་མེད་པའི་རྒྱ་མཚོ།
འཁོར་ལོ་འཁྲུལ་མེད་གཏིང་དུ་འཁྱིལ།
དགའ་སྟོན་བཞིན་པའི་རྒྱ་མཚོ།

Waves of the Infinite

Rest in the vastness, where waves arise,
Where each emotion, each thought, each sigh,
Is but a ripple, a passing flow,
In the boundless ocean, the mind's pure glow.

No need to grasp, no need to flee,
No storm can shake this inner sea.
Anger, joy, and grief appear,
Yet leave no trace, the depths stay clear.

Let the tides of feeling come and go,
Like wind through grass, like silent snow.
No need to fix, no need to change,
Just rest, just breathe, just feel the range.

Awareness wide, without a seam,
No clinging to the passing stream.
From this stillness, action springs,
Effortless, pure, on timeless wings.

No burden to carry, no need to strive,
In this perfect flow, fully alive.
The ocean's heart, the unbounded mind,
Free from the fears that once confined.

So dance, dear heart, in this endless play,
Each moment fresh, each breath a ray.
No shore to reach, no tide to tame,
Just the ocean, forever the same.

Boundless Unity: Beyond Distinctions

When this barrier dissolves, we awaken to **profound unity**—not a merging of all things into one, but the direct realization that everything is **inseparable**.

This unity is expansive, clear, and **spacious**, like galaxies forming in the cosmic dance. It is **uncontrived**, free from conceptual distinctions.

In this **non-dual awareness**, love and compassion arise not as something cultivated, but as a **gravitational force**—binding all beings in effortless connection.

Compassion is not **added** to awareness—it **is** awareness. We no longer see others as separate, but as expressions of the same luminous **presence**.

ཧྲི་བཙུན་གྲིས་བཀའ་སློལ།
ཐེག་པ་དང་པོ་དྲི་བའི་ཞུགས་རིགས་གསལ་འབར་བར་ཤེས།
འོད་དེ་དགའ་གྲོལ་གྱི་རྟོགས་རིག་རྒྱུད་དང་མཉམ།
འཁོར་བ་དང་ཞི་བ་རང་བཞིན་ལ་འཕྲུལ་མ་མེད།
མ་ཡ་དང་རྣམ་པར་སྦྱང་བ་མེད། འོད་ཀྱི་གཞི་ལ་རང་བྱུང་སྐྱེ།
དུས་དང་ས་གཞི་རང་བཞིན་སངས་རྒྱས། ཞི་བ་མ་རགས་དགོས།
སྣང་བའི་ཚུལ་ལ་འཁོར་འགྲོའི་ཟླང་པའི་གཏིང་སྐོར་ཉིད་ཀྱི་སྐོམ་ལས་དཀའ་བ་
མེད། གཞི་ལ་འབད་སྒྲིག་མེད། ངོ་བོར་ལུས་འགོག་པའི་རིགས་མེད།
འཕྲུལ་མའི་ལམ་ནི། གྲོལ་འགྲོའི་རགས་པའི་སྒྲིབ་པ་མེད། ངང་སངས་བཞུགས།
དུས་འདས་པའི་གཉིས་མེད་འགྲོལ་མེད་རང་གི་སྐོར།
འཇིགས་པའི་རྟོགས་པ་མི་འདུག འཕྲུལ་མའི་ལམ་ལ་ཕྱིར་འོངས་པ་ཡང་མི་འདུག
རང་བཞིན་ཀྱི་སྐོར་ལ་རང་གི་སྐོར་དང་འགྲོ།

ཕྱིར་འོངས། —
འདི་ལྟར་དུས་འདས་མེད་ཀྱི་འོད་དང་དམིགས་མེད་ཀྱི་སྐོར་ལ།
བདག་གཞན་མེད། མི་གཅིག་གྱི་ལྟར།
རང་དབང་སྒྲིབ་པ་མེད།

The Practice: Resting in Awareness

Dzogchen teaches that **awakening is immediate**—not something distant or earned, but accessible **here and now**.

Through meditation and mindful presence:

We **rest in pure awareness**, allowing thoughts and emotions to **self-liberate**.

We meet suffering with **openness**, rather than resistance.

We **let go** of grasping, trusting the natural clarity of mind.

As the illusion of separation dissolves, life **opens**—revealing the joy, freedom, and deep interconnectedness of all existence.

We are not fragments, wandering alone. We are luminous threads in a vast, **unfolding mandala**, held together by wisdom and love.

Radiance of rigpa is already here. Simply recognize it.

Awareness of the Light

Master says the first step's clear: Know your pristine, radiant nature here. This light, like quantum's dance so bright, Is Samsara, Nirvana, in each moment's light.

Maya's not rejected, but embraced with grace, Pure being's self-arising in this time and space. Nirvana's not afar, but breath's own core, Cosmic rhythm expanding, forevermore.

The illusion's path? Not escape's harsh plea, But a gentle homecoming, finally free.

Homecoming—

to the infinite universe within,

where all is light, space and joy, all is one, and all is free.

བློ་མཐའ་ཡས་པའི་མཚོ།

གནས། སེམས་འཁོར་བའི་ནང་རང་གཞི་གནས།
གནས། ཆུའི་རྒྱག་དང་མཉམ་པའི་སེམས། རྟོལ་གཏིང་དང་གསལ་བ།
ཕྱིར་བཞུགས། སྣང་བ་གང་འདུག་སེམས་ལ་སྦྲེལ།
གལ་ཏེ་སྤྲིའི་ཆླང་བ་དང་རྒྱག་འདི།
ལོག་པར་མི་འགྲོ། གཉིས་མེད་གྲོལ་མེད།
བྱ་བ་མེད། སྤུར་མེད། རྒྱ་མེད།
ལོག་པར་བསྒོད་པ་མེད། སྤྲོ་བ་མེད།
འཁྲུལ་སྣང་ནི་སྤྲོ་བའི་འཁྲོལ་རྒྱན།
བྱ་བ་མེད། བཞག་ནས་འབར།
ཕྱིར་མེད། གཡོ་མེད།
འགྲོ་མེད། ཉིད་གཉིས་མེད།
འོད་ཀྱི་ཆླང་པ་ལ་འབར།
ཐུགས་རྗེའི་སྒྲིབ་པ་མེད།
མཆིས་པ་འབྱུང་བ། འཁྲོལ་སངས།
ཡིད་སེམས་གྲོལ་མེད།
དེ་གི་རྟོགས་པ་རྣམ་པར་གསལ།
རྣམ་པ་དང་སྒྲ་གཞན་མེད།
ཐུགས་ཀྱི་དབང་དང་མཐའ་མེད།
རྡོ་རྗེ་ཀྱི་འོད་ལ་འབར།

བྱ་བ་མེད། གནས་པ་ཡང་བྱེད་མེད།
བར་འགྲོ་མེད། འགྲོ་མེད།
ཆུ་འདི་དམིགས་མེད་སྟེ།
བདེ་སྐྱིད་རྒྱ་མཚོར་འབབ།
འདུག་གི་ཡང་འགྲོ་མེད།
རླུང་འཁྲུགས་མེད། བཞག་དང་འབབ།
གནས་ནས་གནས། འཁྲུལ་མེད་དུ།
འཁོར་བ་ལས་འབབ།
དུས་ཀྱི་རླུང་པ་ལ་སྤྱོད།
གཞིའི་འབྲས་བུ་སྣ་གཞན་མེད།
གཏིང་དུ་དྲོལ། གནས་ནས་འབབ།

བློ་མཐའ་ཡས་པའི་མཚོ་བཞིན་པ།

A Mind Like a Still Lake

Abide, see the space on every breath!

Abide, the mind like water, calm and clear,

Let go! Reflecting all that may appear.

Each ripple, wave, a passing thought,
Yet nothing lost, and nothing caught.
No doing, no archiving, no explanation,
No expectation. No suffering.
Distorted perception causes suffering.
No doing , just being, just shining
No striving for a distant shore,
No need for less, no need for more.
All things arise, dissolve in place,
Each moment is perfect grace.
A dance of symbols, pure and true,
Yet no distinction—what is new?
The truth, the form, they are the same,
A single flame within the frame.
Blazing nature is beyond explanation.
Without an effort, all is done,
No race to run, no goal begun.

The open sky, the endless sea,
Is just the mind, forever free.

No path to walk, no steps to take,
The mind reflects like a quiet lake.

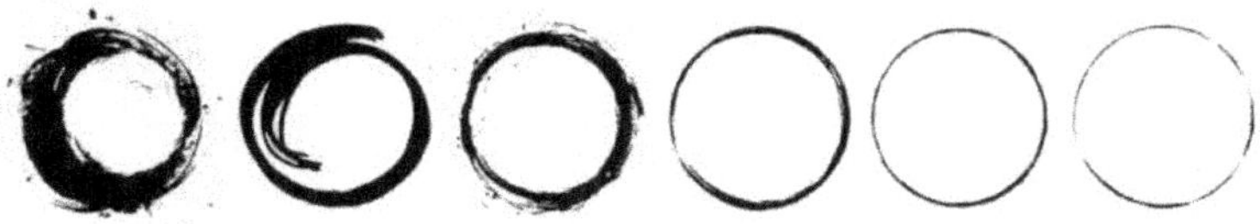

In every breeze, in every glance,
The whole world joins the silent dance.
Let go ! Perfect as it is, unchallenged,

Flow, be free like the wind unchained,

A sacred flow that's never strained.

For nothing lacks, and nothing clings—

A mirror to the endless springs.

Dissolving in the ocean of light,

Doing by not doing ,

Being just being .

Breath, rising

Let go of seeking, searching, try,

For stillness whispers, "Let it lie."

The lake of mind, both vast and still,

It moves with life, yet rests at will.

Commentary

This poem reflects the natural perfection and effortless flow of the mind, as highlighted in the text, likened to the serene reflection of a still lake.

The metaphor of "A Mind Like a Lake" emphasizes the natural, effortless, and clear nature of mind and reality. Also mirror-like mind reflects all and does not get attached, just abides in its radiance.

བློ་མཐའ་ཡས་པའི་མཚོ་བཞིན་པ།

A Mind Like a Still Lake

---

1. བདེན་མེད་ལས་ཐར་པ་ལ།

From illusion to liberation.

Explanation:
In Dzogchen and Mahamudra, recognizing the illusory nature of phenomena leads to liberation. By seeing through the illusion (*བདེན་མེད་, bden med*), one attains freedom (*ཐར་པ་, thar pa*).

Liberation is not found through effort, but through **direct recognition**—seeing the **illusory nature of phenomena** (**bden med**) without clinging, without rejection.

In **Dzogchen and Mahamudra**, this awakening does not arise through analysis but through an **experiential seeing-through**, revealing the **empty, luminous essence** of the mind (**rigpa**).

As Longchenpa describes, this **self-unfolding awareness** is vast, boundless, and effortlessly present— free from conceptual elaboration, resting in its **natural expanse**.

---

2. ནང་ཕྱི་འཇིག་རྟེན་གྱི་འགྱུར་བ།

The universe within and without.

Explanation:
Both internal experiences and external phenomena are manifestations of the same fundamental reality.

In Dzogchen, **inner awareness and outer appearances are inseparable**—expressions of the same primordial ground. Like a **still lake**, the mind remains clear, reflective, and undisturbed, even as ripples of perception arise and fade.

It's a limitless field, alive with the potential for awakening, seeing the world as a **seamless flow**—where distinctions between self and other dissolve in the immediacy of presence.

3. རིག་པའི་རང་བཞིན་རྣམ་རྣལ་གྱི་ཆོས་འབྱུང་།

Is a vast, self-unfolding miracle.

Explanation:
Awareness (རིག་པ་, *rig pa*) naturally manifests all experiences without effort. This spontaneous unfolding is seen as a miraculous display of the mind's nature.

Mind is not a **static reality** but a **miracle unfolding in endless forms**— spontaneously arising, without effort, without contrivance.

This mirrors the Dzogchen principle of **lhun grub** (spontaneous presence) and Mahamudra's recognition of the **natural, uncontrived expression of awareness**.

In **Advaita Vedanta**, nirguna Brahman (formless absolute) this formless ground, though Dzogchen critiques the notion of an eternal essence—preferring **emptiness as freedom**.

4. མཐའ་ཡས་ཀྱི་ཞིང་ཁམས་ལྟ་བུ།

Like the boundless field.

Explanation:
The mind's nature is likened to an infinite field, symbolizing its vastness and openness, free from limitations.

Our beliefs are **constellations in the sky**—transient patterns without substance, projections of conditioned mind. Dzogchen and Mahamudra teach that thoughts are like **clouds drifting**—arising, dissolving, never altering the vast **sky of awareness**.

Zen mirrors this, emphasizing **non-attachment**, while Advaita dissolves ego-identification through **Self-inquiry**.

---

5. ནུས་པ་དང་མཐུན་གྱི་རྒྱུ་མཚན་དང་བཅས།

It is alive with potential.

Explanation:
The mind possesses inherent potential (ནུས་པ་, *nus pa*) for realization and enlightenment, resonating with the concept of Buddha-nature.

Our beliefs are **constellations in the sky**—transient patterns without substance, projections of conditioned mind. Dzogchen and Mahamudra teach that thoughts are like **clouds drifting**—arising, dissolving, never altering the vast **sky of awareness**, natural **non-attachment arising by trusting pure being**, while dissolving ego-identification through **Self-inquiry**.

---

6. རང་གཞན་རང་བྱུང་གི་ཐར་པའི་ལམ་མང་པོ།

Offering infinite pathways to freedom.

Explanation:
There are countless methods and paths leading to liberation, all arising spontaneously from the mind's nature.

The metaphor of the **mind as a mirror and a still lake** expresses its luminous openness. Experiences arise like **ripples or reflections**—never staining, never altering the mirror itself.

This effortless, spontaneous **flow** embodies the Taoist principle of **wu wei** ("doing by not doing")—resonating with Zen's directness and Advaita's boundless unity.

Keith Dowman and Patrul Rinpoche both highlight this truth: **the natural state is already complete—nothing to add, nothing to remove.**

---

7. ངོན་མེད་བསམ་གཏན་གྱི་བསྒྲུམས་རི་མོ།

Our beliefs, those constellations of thought.

Explanation:
Beliefs and conceptual thoughts are like patterns drawn in the sky—lacking inherent substance and permanence.

When the illusion of separateness dissolves, what remains is **boundless unity**— like **stars fusing**, birthing new galaxies.

In this vast interconnectedness, **love and compassion arise spontaneously**—not cultivated, but naturally expressed.

Spontaneous bodhichitta—where awakened compassion flows effortlessly, inseparable from rigpa. Advaita's realization of the Self similarly reveals **universal love beyond ego-boundaries**.

---

8. འདི་ལྟར་འཇིག་རྟེན་གྱི་མཐུན་སྣིག་བཟོས།

Shape our experience of this universe.

Explanation:
Our perceptions and experiences are shaped by these transient thoughts and beliefs, influencing how we engage with the world.

Our notions of reality filed by our rational mind, act as artists, painting the fabric of reality with fleeting patterns— textures of memory, emotions, and thoughts that seem **solid**, yet dissolve upon deeper reflection.

Longchenpa says that **these formations are not the true ground of mind**— they are like **reflections upon water**, ephemeral ripples on the vast expanse of awareness.

---

9. འཆར་བ་འཁྲུགས་པའི་མཁའ་འདྲ་ཞིག་པ་མ་བརྟེན།

But they are the sky itself—when dissolved.

Explanation:

When we release thoughts, dissolve, their **true nature** is revealed— not as obstacles but as **self-liberating appearances**, dissolving into the boundless **sky-like expanse of rigpa**.

Like clouds that form and dissolve effortlessly, these mental projections are never separate from the **clarity of awareness itself**.

This is the essence of Dzogchen— to see thoughts **not as obstructions**, but as **spontaneous movements** arising within luminous space, vanishing without effort or resistance.

---

10. རི་མོ་ལེན་པ་ཞིག་ལ་མཐར་ཕྱིན།

Only patterns we've traced in its expanse.

Explanation:
Our conceptualizations are mere patterns without inherent existence, drawn upon the limitless canvas of the mind.

Thoughts, beliefs, perceptions—they are like brushstrokes upon a vast, unseen canvas. They **appear vividly** yet remain **weightless**, lacking independent existence. Like **ripples upon water** or **clouds drifting across the open sky**, they **form and dissolve**, never altering the boundless clarity beneath.

Dzogchen reveals this truth: ❖ Mental formations are **empty of self-nature** (**rang bzhin med**). ❖ Yet, they manifest **brilliantly** through the **dynamic clarity** (**'od gsal**) of awareness.

To recognize this is to **awaken beyond illusion**—to stop grasping at thoughts and instead **rest effortlessly** in the mind's pristine, unconditioned nature.

---

11. བདེན་མེད་ལས་ཐར་པ་ལ།

From illusion to liberation.

Explanation:
Reiterating the central theme: by recognizing the illusory nature of thoughts and phenomena, one attains liberation.

Liberation does not arise by constructing something new. It unfolds when we **see through**—when we witness that what seemed **solid** was always **a fleeting pattern**, a mirage dissolving into vast openness.

Thar pa (*freedom*) is not achieved through effort, but by unveiling what has always been: a **luminous awareness beyond all conceptual overlays.**

This shift—from confusion to clarity, from suffering to boundless presence— is not a **change** in mind. It is the **recognition** of what mind has always been: **spacious, radiant, free.**

---

12. བདག་གཞན་གི་མཐུན་སྒྲིག་བཟོས།

No path to walk, no steps to take.

Explanation:
In the ultimate view, there is no path or progression—only the direct recognition of the mind's nature.

There is **no journey, no steps, no progression**— Liberation is **not about improving** the mind but recognizing its nature.

Like a **quiet lake**, mind is already **perfect, still, reflective**— not needing alteration, only recognition.

Longchenpa speaks of the **uncontrived nature of reality**, where the effort to seek blocks what is already present. **Stop searching, and the vastness reveals itself.**

---

13. སློ་མཐའ་ཡས་པའི་མཚོ་བཞིན་པ།

The mind reflects like a quiet lake.

Explanation:
A metaphor for the mind's clarity and stillness, reflecting all phenomena without distortion.

In a world filled with distractions, mental clutter, and restless seeking, these teachings **invite us to pause**—to observe, to release.

Through **non-grasping presence**, we discover a **sacred, unstrained flow**— a state where **nothing is lacking, nothing clings, nothing obstructs.**

Even amid the complexities of daily life, we can rest within the awareness that **is always free**— untouched by movement, clear as the open s

14. རླུང་གི་འཕྲིན་ལས་འབྱུང་བ།

In every breeze, in every glance.

Explanation:
Every experience, no matter how subtle, arises from the dynamic play of awareness.

---

15. སྣང་ཆ་མེད་པའི་གནས་སྐབས་ཀྱི་འཁྲུགས་པ།

The whole world joins the silent dance.

Explanation:
All phenomena participate in the silent, effortless dance of existence, beyond conceptual elaboration.

In an age of **constant information, distraction, and noise**, we often mistake mental activity for reality.

These teachings urge us to **pause**, to step beyond fleeting constructs, and to rest in the natural **expanse of pure awareness**.

Observe your thoughts—they are clouds, not sky.

Release attachment—see patterns, but do not cling.

Rest in awareness—not chasing, not resisting, simply **being**.

---

16. འགྲོ་བའི་ལམ་མེད་པ།

Let go! Perfect as it is, unchallenged.

Explanation:
Encouragement to release grasping and accept reality as it is—perfect and complete.

Our minds are **like infinite canvases**, where appearances arise and disappear, where patterns come and go.

But the canvas itself—**vast, empty, radiant**—remains untouched.

Liberation is **not** about reshaping the images. It is about recognizing their **insubstantial nature**— and resting, effortlessly, in the **timeless expanse of awareness itself**.

✨ **Nothing to chase. Nothing to hold. Only the vast clarity of being.**

---

17. རླུང་གི་འཕྲིན་ལས་འབྱུང་བ།

Flow, be free like the wind unchained.

Explanation:
Embrace the freedom and spontaneity of awareness, unbound like the wind.

All phenomena arise and dissolve within awareness, **naturally, effortlessly, without struggle**.

Action becomes **"doing by not doing,"** being is simply **being**—free from grasping.

This principle of **wu wei**, found in Taoism, resonates deeply with Dzogchen— spontaneous action flowing from pure presence, unforced and uncontrived.

---

18. གསལ་བའི་འབྱུང་བ་མ་བརྟེན་པ།

A sacred flow that's never strained.

Explanation:
The natural expression of the mind's clarity flows effortlessly, without contrivance.

Clarity (**gsal ba**) expresses itself **naturally**—there's no need to push, force, or fabricate anything. This is the essence of **lhun grub** (*natural perfection*): enlightened qualities manifest **spontaneously** when we stop interfering.

Imagine a river flowing effortlessly to the sea—this is mind **unobstructed, uncontrived, free**. Such as a river flowing effortlessly to the sea—this is mind **unobstructed, uncontrived, free**.

19. མེད་པ་མེད་པའི་མཚན་ཉིད་ལ།

For nothing lacks, and nothing clings.

Explanation:

In the state of **non-duality**, there is no sense of **deficiency** or **grasping**—awareness is **already complete**, like the sky untouched by passing clouds.

We spend our lives trying to **fill an imagined void**—chasing goals, relationships, identity—but Dzogchen reveals:

❖ Nothing was ever missing.

❖ Nothing needs to be held onto.

Like breath moving in and out, life **flows effortlessly** when we stop clutching at illusions.

20. མེ་ཏོག་མེ་ཏོག་གི་མཚན་ཉིད་ལ།

A mirror to the endless springs.

Explanation:

The mind is **a flawless mirror**—it reflects everything, yet remains unstained. Represents all phenomena without bias.

This is **rigpa**—awareness that simply **sees**, without judgment, without struggle, effortlessly reflecting the **flow of experience**.

Think of a crystal-clear lake: ❖ Joy arises—it reflects. ❖ Sorrow comes—it reflects. ❖ Nothing sticks. Nothing stains.

---

21. འོད་ཀྱི་རྒྱ་མཚོའི་ནང་དུ་འབྱུང་བ།

Dissolving in the ocean of light.

Explanation:
All phenomena dissolve into the luminous expanse of awareness, the ocean of light.

Everything—thoughts, emotions, perceptions— ultimately **dissolves** into the luminous space of awareness, just as **rivers merge into the ocean**.

This **ocean of light** is the **boundless ground of being**— always present, always open, always free.

22. མ་བྱེད་པའི་བྱ་བ་ལ།

Doing by not doing.

Explanation:
Effortless action— Doing arises naturally without deliberate effort—a key principle in non-dual traditions.

Instead of **forcing** decisions, movements, or responses, we let **wisdom and compassion** guide us—naturally, spontaneously.

❖ A skilled dancer does not **think** about every step— they move **with the rhythm** of presence.

❖ A musician does not force a melody— they let the song unfold.

23. ཡོད་པ་ཡོད་པའི་མཚན་ཉིད་ལ།

Being just being.

Explanation:
Abiding in the natural state of being, Abiding in **the natural state** is **simple**—resting in awareness without modification; free from conceptual overlays.

No need to **fix** the mind, no need to **reshape reality**. Presence is **already perfect** when left alone.

24. དབུས་མའི་འཁོར་ལོ་ལ།

Breath, rising.

Explanation:
Observing the breath as a manifestation of the present moment, anchoring awareness.

Even the breath is a manifestation of **pure awareness**— a gentle anchor to the **here and now**.

It rises, falls, disappears, returns— without control, without effort.

25. འཚོལ་བ་འཚོལ་བའི་མཚན་ཉིད་ལ།

Let go of seeking, searching, try.

Explanation:
Release the habitual tendencies of seeking and striving; rest in natural awareness.

The **Dzogchen path** is not about **seeking enlightenment** or **striving for perfection**.

Realization comes from **letting go**— from **resting** in effortless, luminous presence.

Dzogchen Meditation: Breath as the Path to Spacious Awareness

Breath: From Sky to Heart Rest in openness, allowing your breath to flow effortlessly like the vast expanse of space. Inhale, sensing how luminous energy—pure and uncontrived—descends from the infinite sky through the crown of your head. It moves effortlessly along your central channel, dissolving barriers until it merges into the radiant presence of your heart.

Breathing in, feel the breath not as air but as light, as boundless awareness entering your being. It is not something separate—no effort, no expectation—just a seamless unfolding of presence. Breathe through the heart or through the luminous pores of your skin, expanding infinitely into spacious awareness.

Now, **drop all concepts**. The sky is not outside; it is your own vast, luminous nature. Not something to visualize, but something to **be**. Spacious, timeless, effortless. The sun shines without agenda, permeating all without preference. This light—**self-arising, self-illuminating**—is none other than the natural radiance of awareness itself. It does not need to be created; it is already here.

Nothing is obstructed. Nothing is missing. Fulfillment is not found elsewhere—it resides everywhere, uncontrived, untouched by striving.

Meditation: The Mind as Guru

Rest in "I Am All" Take a breath—not to grasp, not to control, but simply to settle in the vast expanse that already exists. Whisper inwardly, **"I am everything"**, or **"I am That"**, and then let go. No need to repeat, no need to do—just **be**. Who am I?

Do not seek an answer. Do not chase after thoughts or sensations. Instead, surrender into the unfiltered presence that naturally arises. Recognize that **nothing needs to be changed**—the pure essence of Being, vast and luminous, is already complete.

Go to the heart, resting without distraction. Not focusing, not meditating in the conventional sense—simply letting mind unfold as itself. The pure consciousness that is always present **reveals itself spontaneously** as the vast and limitless expanse of awareness. No need to refine or alter anything—there is nothing to improve, nothing to grasp, nothing to perfect.

All merges. The inside and the outside dissolve—the boundary between observer and observed no longer holds meaning. There is only **presence**, flowing naturally, radiant in its own completeness.

Spiritual practice is not an effort to acquire something external, but a **release of the mind's divisions**. When we do not chase after thoughts, we discover that there is no "I" that meditates, no object of meditation—only vast openness, unobstructed awareness. The flow of Being itself, free from all limitations.

To **step beyond duality** is not to find something new, but to see what has always been—the undivided nature of mind. Here, the concept of inside or outside vanishes. The illusion of separation dissolves. There is only **this**, the infinite space of presence, the timeless now that exists without effort, without struggle.

Practice:

- Relax **deeply** into the present without controlling or manipulating experience.
- Do not chase after thoughts or resist emotions—allow everything to arise and dissolve effortlessly.
- Rest in the luminous expanse where awareness is **self-illuminating, timeless, and free.**

Let all striving cease. Surrender fully, not as an act of will but as a natural unfolding into **the infinite, sky-like nature of mind itself.** Nothing to reach. Nothing to become. Only vastness, only presence—already complete, already whole.

རིག་པའི་རྣམ་བཤད་དང་གཞི།

Key Concepts and Aspects of Rigpa in Dzogchen

Rigpa (རིག་པ་) is the pristine awareness that is primordially pure, spontaneously present, and beyond conceptual limitations. Longchenpa's teachings emphasize its effortless nature, guiding practitioners toward direct recognition of their true essence.

ཀ་དག། — Primordial Purity (Ka-dag, ཀ་དག་)

- Rigpa is primordially pure, meaning it is empty of inherent existence and untouched by defilements.
- This purity is not something to be attained but rather recognized as the natural state of mind, beyond concepts of "pure" and "impure".
- It is likened to the sky—unchanging and unconditioned, serving as the ground (Gzhi, གཞི་) for all phenomena.

ལྷུན་གྲུབ། — Spontaneous Presence (Lhun-drub, ལྷུན་གྲུབ་)

- Rigpa is not a static void but a dynamic presence with innate qualities like luminosity and compassion.
- Longchenpa describes it as "effortless, uncontrived, and beyond conditions," akin to sunlight illuminating the sky.
- These qualities manifest naturally without cause or effort.

འོད་གསལ་སྦྱོར་ཡུག། — Unity of Emptiness and Clarity (Od-sal Song-yug, འོད་གསལ་སྦྱོར་ཡུག་)

- Emptiness (śūnyatā) and clarity (gsal-ba) are inseparable in Rigpa.
- Emptiness is the ground from which luminous awareness arises, like clouds dissolving in the sky.
- Longchenpa articulates this as the "indivisible union" forming the essence of mind.

རང་བྱུང་ཡེ་ཤེས། — Self-Arising Wisdom (Rang-byung Yeshe, རང་བྱུང་ཡེ་ཤེས་)

- Wisdom in Rigpa is not acquired but arises spontaneously from pure awareness.
- This natural intelligence transcends intellectual analysis and is revealed through practices like Trekchö (Cutting Through Delusion, ཁྲེགས་ཆོད་).

གཞི། — The Ground (Gzhi, གཞི་)

- The ground is the basis of both samsara and nirvana, synonymous with Rigpa.
- Recognizing it as one's true nature is key to liberation.
- Longchenpa equates it with the "primordial glow" (Ye gdangs, ཡེ་གདངས་) underlying all phenomena.

སེམས་ཉིད། — The Nature of Mind (Sem-nyid, སེམས་ཉིད་)

- Longchenpa uses Sem-nyid interchangeably with Rigpa, describing it as "primordially pure, spontaneously present, and the unity of emptiness and clarity".
- Ordinary mind (Sems, སེམས་) is a contraction of this natural state.

བདེ་བ་མེད་པ། — Effortless Being

- Abiding in Rigpa requires no striving.

- Longchenpa's Trekchö (ཁྲེགས་ཆོད་) emphasizes resting in "natural meditation," allowing thoughts to self-liberate without manipulation.

རང་གྲོལ། — Self-Liberation (Rang-grol, རང་གྲོལ་)

- Delusions dissolve when recognized as empty manifestations of Rigpa.
- Garab Dorje's third principle highlights this "confidence in liberation," as thoughts arise and dissolve naturally.

རིག་པའི་ལམ་རྣམས། — Aspects of the Dzogchen Path

ངོ་སྤྲོད། — Direct Introduction (Ngo-tro, ངོ་སྤྲོད་)

- A qualified master introduces the student to Rigpa through pointing-out instructions, enabling immediate recognition.
- This transmission is central to Garab Dorje's teachings.

ཁྲེགས་ཆོད། — Cutting Through (Trekchö, ཁྲེགས་ཆོད་)

- This practice involves settling into Rigpa by cutting through mental obscurations.
- Longchenpa's Trekchö instructions emphasize effortless rest in awareness.

ཐོད་རྒལ། — Leaping Over (Tögal, ཐོད་རྒལ་)

- Advanced practitioners use visionary experiences of light to realize Dharmakaya (ཆོས་སྐུ་).
- Jigme Lingpa and Longchenpa consider this the pinnacle of Dzogchen meditation.

གསུམ་པའི་སྐུ། — Three Kayas (Trikaya, སྐུ་གསུམ་)

- Dharmakaya (ཆོས་སྐུ་) — Empty essence.
- Sambhogakaya (ལོངས་སྐུ་) — Luminous expression.
- Nirmanakaya (སྤྲུལ་སྐུ་) — Compassionate manifestation.

དམ་ཚིག་བཞི། — Four Samayas (དམ་ཚིག་བཞི་)

Commitments guiding Dzogchen practice:

1. **Ineffability**
2. **Openness**
3. **Spontaneous presence**
4. **Oneness**

རིག་པའི་སྦྱོན་མ། — Integration into Daily Life

- If we want to accomplish enlightenment it's not enough to meditate , mornings and evenings, we need to meditate all day long and be aware when we sleep. Great perfection stresses embodying Rigpa in all activities, transforming mundane actions into expressions of wisdom.

རིག་པའི་བརྡར་བ། — Longchenpa's Contributions

Longchenpa systematized Dzogchen philosophy, integrating it with Buddhist scholasticism. His works, like the Trilogy of Natural Freedom and Nyingthig Yabshi, clarify Rigpa's nature and path, positioning Dzogchen as the pinnacle of Buddhist practice.

Integrating Dzogchen and Non-Dual Traditions in Modern Life

Direct Recognition rigpa mirrors direct experience.

Spontaneity and Compassion Liberation **is not distant**—it arises spontaneously when we dissolve illusion, awakening to **universal love** as the binding force.

No Path, Just Resting There is no **path to walk or steps to take**—only resting in the **mind's nature as it is**.

Nothing to Fix, Nothing to Chase

When striving ceases, clarity **unfolds effortlessly**.

The **mind-mirror reflects all**, yet clings to nothing. Thoughts **arise and dissolve**, never altering the **luminous ground**.

In today's fast-paced world, **let go of conceptual clutter**, rest in **open awareness**, and cultivate **compassion— transforming mental samsara into the dance of awakening**.

Pause instead of striving—allow awareness to reveal itself naturally.

Observe without judgment—thoughts are clouds, you are the sky.

Let emotions arise and dissolve—like waves, never separate from the ocean.

Act from clarity—not from effort, but from deep presence.

This is the essence of **doing by not doing**, the **fantastic flow of true nature**, the **completion already present**.

✨ **Rest. Recognize. Be. This is freedom.**

ཁྲེགས་ཆོད། — Cutting Through Delusion (Trekchö) in Dzogchen

Definition and Meaning

Trekchö (ཁྲེགས་ཆོད་, khregs chod) literally means "cutting through solidity" or "spontaneous cutting of tension." It is a foundational Dzogchen practice aimed at directly severing the root of delusion by recognizing the empty and luminous nature of thoughts and emotions as they arise. This recognition leads to resting in Rigpa, pure, non-dual awareness free from conceptual elaboration.

Malcolm Smith poetically compares Trekchö to "an undone bundle," like a hay bale with its twine cut—symbolizing the effortless unraveling of mental fabrications. Vimalamitra defines it as: > "The system of buddhahood through immediate liberation as a directly perceived realization not connected to appearances."

ལྟ་བ་དང་སྤྱོད་པ། — Core Practice

The essence of Trekchö is resting in the natural state of mind, without striving, manipulation, or contrivance. The central instruction is:

> "This instant freshness, unspoiled by the thoughts of the three times; you directly see in actuality by letting be in naturalness."

Practitioners first receive pointing-out instructions from a qualified master, enabling direct recognition of Rigpa. The practice involves:

- Recognizing thoughts and emotions as empty, luminous appearances that self-liberate when not grasped or rejected.
- Settling effortlessly into open, objectless awareness.
- Avoiding deliberate effort to control or alter experience.

Chögyam Trungpa Rinpoche describes Trekchö as "cutting any experientially inclined trips," emphasizing its directness and immediacy.

འབྲེལ་བའི་སྤྱོད་པ། — Relationship to Other Practices

Trekchö is often considered the Dzogchen equivalent of Mahamudra and Shikantaza (just sitting) in Zen, all emphasizing nondual awareness and effortless presence. It serves as the preliminary and essential practice before advancing to Tögal (leaping over, ཐོད་རྒལ་), which uses visionary yogic techniques to realize the Dharmakaya.

ཡིད་ཆེས་དང་རྟོག་དཔྱད། — Stages and Instructions

Jigme Lingpa classifies Trekchö instructions into:

1. Ordinary instructions: Reject conceptual elaborations of emptiness.
2. Extraordinary instructions: Establish the view, address doubts, and cultivate the "four ways of being at leisure"—
    - Mountainlike view,
    - Oceanlike meditation,
    - Skillful activity,
    - Unconditional result.

The practitioner rests in the present moment of Rigpa, avoiding extremes of existence and nonexistence, cultivating effortless abiding in the natural state.

མངོན་སྟོང་དང་སྤྱོད་པ། — Practical Guidance

- Posture and Focus: Maintain relaxed, open awareness; eyes may be open or closed.
- Use of the "Phat" Syllable: A sharp sound used to refresh and return to openness when distracted.
- Awareness of Thoughts: Allow thoughts to arise and dissolve naturally without interference, recognizing their empty nature.

འགྲོ་བའི་ཆོས་དང་འབྲེལ་བ། — Effects and Benefits

Trekchö practice leads to:

- The collapse of the entire edifice of delusion, revealing primordial purity and simplicity.
- Increasing gaps between thoughts and dissipation of emotional disturbances.
- Spontaneous self-liberation of mental events, without suppression or transformation.

- Recognition of the natural state as the basis for liberation.

ཐོད་རྒལ། — Leaping Over (Tögal): The Complementary Advanced Practice

Tögal (Tib. ཐོད་རྒལ་, thod rgal) means "leaping over" or "direct crossing." It is an advanced Dzogchen practice that uses visionary experiences of light and energy to realize the Dharmakaya, or truth body.

ཆོས་སྣའི་སྡེ། — Key Features

- Practiced typically in darkness or through sky gazing.
- Engages subtle body channels, winds, and drops to generate spontaneous luminous visions (thigles, ཐིག་ལེ་).
- Progresses through four visionary stages, culminating in the exhaustion of phenomena in dharmata (absolute nature).
- Requires stability in Trekchö before initiation.

རྣམ་བཤད། — Purpose and Outcome

Tögal enables practitioners to:

- Bypass ordinary conceptual mind and directly experience nondual reality.
- Attain realization of the three kayas (Dharmakaya, Sambhogakaya, Nirmanakaya) within one lifetime.
- Shed physical and karmic limitations without physical death.
- Merge with the primordial radiance of awareness, stabilizing spontaneous presence and compassion.

བདེ་གཤེགས་ཀྱི་གདན་སྟོང་དང་སྤྱོད་པ། — Practice Requirements

- Direct introduction and guidance from a qualified teacher.
- Strong discipline and retreat conditions.
- Maintenance of firm posture and specific gazes to prevent dispersion of vital energies.

དངོས་གཞི། — Summary

Practice	Description	Outcome

Trekchö (ཁྲེགས་ཆོད་)	Cutting through delusion by resting effortlessly in the empty, luminous nature of mind (Rigpa).	Collapse of delusion; spontaneous self-liberation; recognition of primordial purity.
Tögal (ཐོད་རྒལ་)	Visionary practice using light and subtle energies to realize Dharmakaya directly.	Direct realization of Buddha bodies; rapid attainment of enlightenment; merging with radiance.

Together, Trekchö and Tögal form the complete Dzogchen path, guiding practitioners from direct recognition of awareness to full embodiment of enlightened wisdom and compassion.

Bringing Trekchö into Daily Life

1. Resting in Natural Awareness – Instead of engaging in mental struggle, simply notice the space in which thoughts arise and dissolve. Let awareness be expansive, like the sky.
2. Recognizing Thoughts as Empty – Whether you're working, conversing, or relaxing, recognize thoughts as luminous yet insubstantial appearances—they self-liberate when not grasped.
3. Letting Go of Effort – Avoid striving to manipulate your state of mind. The more naturally you relax into presence, the more Rigpa remains accessible.

Practicing Tögal in Everyday Experience

1. Gazing at the Sky – If possible, spend time under an open sky. Allow its vastness to reflect your mind's limitless nature.
2. Awareness of Light – Pay attention to light sources—sunlight, reflections, and even the inner luminosity of awareness itself. Visionary practice can begin with simply noticing how light interacts with space.

3. Perceiving Reality as Radiant Energy – Tögal points to the spontaneous manifestation of Rigpa. Whether in meditation or movement, recognize the vibrancy within all phenomena.

Effortless Presence in Action

- Whether walking, eating, working, or engaging with others, hold awareness openly.
- Notice spontaneous clarity and compassion arising from within Rigpa.
- Instead of controlling experience, allow reality to unfold naturally.

གསུམ་པའི་སྐུ། — The Three Kayas (Trikaya) in Dzogchen

Longchenpa, one of the foremost Dzogchen masters, explains the Three Kayas (Trikaya)—Dharmakaya, Sambhogakaya, and Nirmanakaya—not as separate entities but as inherent, inseparable aspects of our own primordial nature (Rigpa, རིག་པ་). This teaching aligns with the broader Mahayana Buddhist doctrine, which elucidates the multidimensional nature of Buddhahood as a unified reality manifesting in different modes.

1. ཆོས་སྐུ། — Dharmakaya (Truth Body)

- Represents the ultimate, unmanifested reality—the essence of Rigpa.
- Beyond form, concept, and duality, embodying the absolute nature of Buddha mind.
- The ground from which all phenomena arise and the source of all enlightened activity.
- Primordial purity (Ka-dag, ཀ་དག་)—emptiness that underlies everything and is the ultimate truth recognized in Dzogchen practice.

2. ལོངས་སྐུ། — Sambhogakaya (Enjoyment Body)

- The radiant, blissful expression of Rigpa, manifesting as luminous, divine forms.
- Functions as the body of communication between enlightened beings and advanced practitioners.

- Through Sambhogakaya, enlightened mind manifests as the five wisdoms and the play of compassionate energy.
- Bridges the formless Dharmakaya and the physical world, representing the dynamic qualities of awareness.

3. སྤྲུལ་སྐུ། — Nirmanakaya (Emanation Body)

- The manifestation body that appears in the everyday world to benefit sentient beings.
- Includes historical Buddhas, spiritual teachers, and any form that arises from compassion to aid others.
- The tangible expression of Rigpa's compassionate activity within samsara.

གསུམ་པའི་སྐུ་གཞི་དང་འབྲེལ་བ། — Unified Nature of the Three Kayas

In Dzogchen, these three kayas are understood as aspects of the same primordial ground:

- Essence (Dharmakaya) — The fundamental emptiness and purity of mind.
- Nature (Sambhogakaya) — The spontaneous radiance and clarity.
- Capacity (Nirmanakaya) — The compassionate manifestation in the world.

Everything perceived externally corresponds to Nirmanakaya; the underlying luminous energy is Sambhogakaya; and the ultimate truth is Dharmakaya. These are not separate realities but different expressions of the same fundamental nature.

ལམ་དང་འབྲེལ་བ། — The Path and Fruition

- As a path, the three kayas manifest as bliss, clarity, and non-thought.
- As a fruition, they are the full realization of Buddhahood in its three bodies.
- Advanced Dzogchen practice, especially Tögal (Leaping Over, ཐོད་རྒལ་), is said to bring about the rapid realization of these three kayas within a single lifetime.

དམ་ཚིག་བཞི། — The Four Foundational Commitments (Samayas) in Dzogchen

Longchenpa highlights four great samayas as essential commitments guiding Dzogchen practitioners. These samayas are spiritual principles that shape understanding and conduct on the path of the Great Perfection (Dzogchen, རྫོགས་ཆེན་).

1. མི་བརྗོད་དང་མི་འདྲུས། — Ineffability (Non-Existence / Non-Conceptuality)

- The natural samaya of abiding in the primordially pure essence of awareness, beyond all elaboration.
- Nothing needs to be maintained; the practitioner simply rests in spontaneous presence.
- Represents abiding in the primordial wisdom of emptiness.

2. རང་བཞིན་གྱི་སྟོང་པ་ཉམས་མེད། — Openness (Evenness)

- Transcending fixation on conditioned phenomena by resting in their actual nature without attachment.
- The five sense consciousnesses rest in the realization of suchness, free from grasping to inner or outer objects.
- Primordial awareness abiding as natural evenness.

3. རང་བྱུང་གི་སྣང་བ། — Spontaneous Presence

- Remaining within the quality of knowing and open radiance of suchness.
- The profusion of qualities arises naturally and spontaneously, independent of deliberate practice.
- This samaya involves recognizing awareness as the natural ground from which everything arises.

4. གཅིག་པའི་ཡེ་ཤེས། — Oneness

- Abiding in the singular wisdom beyond words, where all conceptual distinctions dissolve into unity.
- Recognizing that everything is perfect within the single basis of primordial wisdom.

དམ་ཚིག་དང་རིག་པའི་འབྲེལ་བ། — The Role of Samaya in Dzogchen Practice

- Samaya (དམ་ཚིག་, dam tshig) generally refers to vows or commitments taken upon empowerment in Vajrayana Buddhism.

- In Dzogchen, samayas are not merely ethical vows but reflect the direct experience of the ultimate nature—that all phenomena are visible, audible, and aware emptiness.
- Longchenpa's Precious Treasury of the Way of Abiding elaborates on these four uncommon samayas as the modes of abiding in the Great Perfection.
- There are also extensive lists of root and branch samayas guiding gradual practitioners, emphasizing the importance of maintaining harmony with the truth of Rigpa.

སེམས་ཀྱི་གར།

སེམས་ཀྱི་གར་གྱི་ནང་གང་བྱུང་།
བསམ་པ་འོག་མི་འགྲུབ། དུས་ཀྱི་གནས་སྐབས་སུ།
གཞོན་པ་མེད་པའི་བྱང་སེམས། སྤྲོས་པ་མེད་པའི་དངོས་སུ་གཞི།
བྱང་སེམས་ལྷུན་གྲུབ་འོད་ཀྱི་སྣང་བ་བཞིན།
གཞོན་མེད། དམིགས་པ་མེད། བཞག་ནས་འབར།
རང་གི་སྒྲོན་མེད་འོད་ཀྱི་སྣང་བ་དང་མཉམ།

རང་བྱུང་སྒྲོང་བ་རང་གི་གནས།
རང་བྱུང་གནས་སྐབས་དང་མཉམ།
འགྲོ་མེད། འགྲུབ་མེད། འཁོར་ལས་འདོད་འཁོར་མེད།
རང་བྱུང་བཞིན་གྱི་གཞི་རང་དབང་རང་དོན།
བསམ་པ་ལས་འགྲོ་མེད། གཟུགས་གྱི་གཟུགས་མེད།
འཁོར་བ་རང་དབང་གི་གནས།

འབར་བ་དང་གཉིས་མེད་གྱི་རྡོ་རྗེ།
བསམ་པ་སེམས་ལས་འདོད་མེད།
དགོན་པ་དང་བསྒྱུར་བ་མེད། འཁོར་ལས་འཁོར་མེད།
རང་བྱུང་རང་འདོད་འདོད་མེད། འཁོར་ལས་འཁོར་མེད།

རང་གི་དངོས་པོ་བྱང་སེམས་དང་མཉམ།
ལྷུང་བ་མེད། འཁོར་ལས་འཁོར་མེད།
བསམ་པ་མེད། འགྲོ་མེད།
གནས་མེད། འབར་མེད། འཁོར་ལས་འཁོར་མེད།

རང་གི་བདག་འབར་དང་མཉམ།
རྡོ་རྗེ་བཞིན་གྱི་འབར་བ།
རྡོ་རྗེ་ཀྱི་གནས་ན་མི་གནས།
རང་བྱུང་འཁོར་ལས་འཁོར་མེད།
གཞིའི་འབྲས་བུ་སླ་གཞན་མེད།

འགྲོ་མེད། གནས་མེད། འབར་མེད།
དུས་སུ་འབར་བ་མེད།
འགྲོ་མེད། འཁོར་ལས་འཁོར་མེད།
ལྷུང་བ་མེད། འཁོར་ལས་འཁོར་མེད།
བསམ་པ་མེད། འབར་མེད།
གནས་ནས་འབར། འཁོར་ལས་འཁོར་མེད།

དུས་ཀྱི་ཆླང་པ་ལ་སྤྱོད།
རང་གི་སྨྲོན་མེད་འོད་ཀྱི་སྣང་བ།
རང་གི་རང་གནས་དང་མཉམ།
རང་གི་བདག་འབར་དང་མཉམ།
གཏིང་དུ་རྡོལ། གནས་ནས་འབར།

Dance of mind

In the dance of mind, we find our state,

Where thoughts arise, yet never late,

Like clouds that drift in sky so wide,

Our consciousness, a perfect guide.

Effortless presence, pure and bright,
Spontaneity flows, like morning light,
No force, no strain, just pure intent,
In each moment, truly present.

Intrinsic perfection, all things hold,
Spontaneity, in wisdom bold,
Let go of striving, trust the flow,
In nature's truth, we softly glow.

Non-contrivance, life as it seems,
Embrace the flow, like gentle streams,
Without imposing fears or doubt,
Our true self shines, within, without.

Self-liberation, thoughts set free,
Arise, dissolve, like waves at sea,

No traces left, attachments fade,

In freedom's light, we're gently swayed.

Great completeness, Dzogchen's way,

Experience pure, without delay,

The primordial state, we realize,

With no concepts, the truth belies.

Unified experience, none apart,

Observer, observed, one in heart,

The non-dual nature, clearly shown,

In unity, we're never alone.

Joy and ease, in each breath found,

Actions flow, without a bound,

Open mind, relaxed and clear,

In this space, no need to fear.

Thoughts like leaves on rivers drift,
Emotions rise, but then they lift,
Our mind, a lake, so tranquil, deep,
Disturbances but ripples sleep.

Waves of ocean, rise and fall,
Depth serene, embraces all,
Birds through sky, they come and go,
Yet sky remains, its endless glow.
Wind of feelings, fleeting breeze,
Air unchanged, in endless ease,
Vast mountain peak, clouds float on by,
Leaving no trace, against the sky.

Shadows dance, yet light remains,

Essence pure, through life's domains,
Weather changes, sky stays bright,
Constancy in day and night.

Bubbles in the stream, so brief,
Mind's deep well, holds no grief,
Reflections pass, yet depth stays clear,
In stillness found, we persevere.

In this life,
truths entwine,
and wisdom shine,
we come to see,
The unity of you and me.

རྫོགས་ཆེན་དང་མ་སྦྱར་བའི་ཆོས་ལུགས་དང་ཐྲུབ་ཐོབ་འགྲོ་བ།

Integrating Dzogchen and Non-Dual Traditions in Modern Life

Dzogchen, often hailed as the **"Great Perfection" or "Great Completeness"**, represents the **zenith** of the Nyingma school of Tibetan Buddhism, offering a **direct** and **profound pathway** to realizing the **primordial nature of mind**.

This ancient tradition posits that **our essential being**—akin to **Buddha nature**—is **inherently pure, complete, and already enlightened** from the very beginning. This **fundamental truth** is **not attained through arduous practice**, but rather **an intrinsic reality awaiting recognition.**

The **ultimate aim of Dzogchen** is to **uncover and dwell** within this **foundational ground of existence**, a realm that **transcends the limitations of our ordinary, conceptual mind.**

རྫོགས་ཆེན་དང་མ་སྦྱར་བའི་ཆོས་ལུགས། —

Dzogchen in the Landscape of Non-Dual Traditions

Dzogchen aligns closely with **non-dual philosophies**, which emphasize the **fundamental interconnectedness and unity of all reality.** This **dissolves the perceived separations** between **self and other, subject and object.**

1. Similarities with Other Non-Dual Traditions

- **Advaita Vedanta** describes the **ultimate reality as Brahman**, beyond duality.
- **Zen Buddhism** emphasizes **direct experience beyond conceptualization.**

- **Dzogchen's uniqueness lies in its Buddhist understanding** of **emptiness (Shunyata) and the innate luminosity of mind.**

2. Distinctions in Methodology

Although these traditions **converge on direct realization**, Dzogchen presents a **unique ontological view**, emphasizing:

- **The unity of emptiness (Ka-dag, ཀ་དག་) and spontaneous presence (Lhun-drub, ལྷུན་གྲུབ་).**
- **The self-liberating quality of awareness** through **Rang-grol (རང་གྲོལ་)**—spontaneous liberation of thoughts.
- **Transmission through direct introduction** (*Ngo-tro,* ངོ་སྤྲོད་) rather than progressive realization.

ཚུལ་མེད་དང་གཉིད་ཟབ། — Practical Wisdom for the Modern World

Modern life is **marked by relentless pace, overwhelming information, and fragmentation**. Dzogchen's **core principles** offer **powerful antidotes** to stress, anxiety, and alienation.

1. Radical Self-Acceptance Over Striving

- **Challenges modern obsession** with **constant self-improvement** and seeking external validation.
- Encourages **a radical acceptance of ourselves as already complete and whole.**

2. Present-Moment Awareness as a Sanctuary

- Dzogchen focuses on **cultivating effortless presence** and **uncontrived relaxation.**
- Provides **a refuge from mental agitation and anxiety.**

རྒྱ་མཚོའི་འཕྱུར་འཁྲུག

རྒྱ་མཚོའི་སྨད་ཁའི་གཙང་དག་ཡིན་པར།
འོད་གསལ་གྱི་འཕྱུར་འཁྲུག་གསང་བའི་སྟོན་པ།
དུས་ཡུན་མེད་པའི་འོད་དང་འཁྲུག་པ།
ང་དང་ཁྱེད་རང་ནང་ཡང་འོད་དང་འཁྲུག་པ།

བདེན་པ་ལེན་མི་འགོལ་ཡང་མི་འཆི།
ཁྱེད་རང་གི་ནང་བཞིན་གྱི་གནས་ཚུལ་གྲོངས་ཡོད།

བདག་གི་སྣ་ལྷུན་བཞིན་ཡོད་པར་རང་བཞིན་གི་བརྗོད་པ།
རྣམ་པར་རྗོད་པའི་གནས་ཚུལ་རྟོགས་པ།

བརྟགས་ན་རང་བཞིན་ལ་འཇུག་གཏོང་ན།
གཙང་དག་བཞིན་དུ་ཤེས་ན་རྒྱ་རྩོད་མེད།

བདེན་པ་འཚོལ་ན་རིགས་ཀྱི་སྣང་བ་འགྲུབ།
ནམ་མཁའ་རྒྱ་ཆེན་པའི་འདི་ནང་འདོད་པ།
འཛིན་པ་གཏོར་ན་སྣ་དག་པའི་རྒྱ་ཆེན་པ།
གཟུགས་ཀྱི་རྟོགས་པ་ནང་གསལ་ཤིང་བཟང་པོ།

བསྒོད་མི་བརྟགས་པར་སྒོང་ཞིང་ཡིན།
དུས་མི་སྒོང་ན་ཉམས་མེད་པ།
འཁྲུགས་འཁྲུག་དང་བཙོས་པ་གསོལ་ནི།

ང་ལ་བདེན་པའི་སྣ་བཞིན་གྱི་སྙིང་རྗེ་སྤྲོས་མེད་མཛད་མཁན་ལ།

རྒྱ་མཚོའི་འཕྱུར་འཁྲུག།

Ocean Waves

In the depths of the ocean, where purity resides

Luminous waves dance, with secrets they confide

Edges glistening, with an eternal glow

All-pervading sunshine, through me and through you through me and through you

When the truth is lost, but never truly dies

Your inner self rises, reaching for the skies reachin' for the skies

When my body is left behind, my essence lives on

Divine nature, everlasting, forever strong forever strong

When lost, come back home to our indestructible essence,

aging does not exist when pure nature is realized.

In the search for truth, we wander far and wide

Underneath a sky that stretches out so wide

But when the compass fails and we lose our way

It's in our core, where we find solace and stay

Oh, come back home to the unfading self come back home

Where time stands still and love can freely help

Brush away the illusions that cloud your view

Ageing dissolves when pure nature shines through

དེ་དགོངས་པའི་བདེན་སྒྲུལ་གྱི་སྒོ་སྒྲིག ཞི་བའི་སྒོ་ལ་གང་ཡང་མེད་པའི་དཀའ་བ
ཞི་བ་དང་དང་དྭ་སྒྲོལ་བའི་འོད་འབར་བ
དགའ་བའི་མཛེས་མོ་དང་འཁོར་བའི་ཚུལ་རིགས་ལྡན་པ
སློ་བའི་རང་ངོ་རེ་བར་དགོས་པ་ལས་འོངས་པ
འོད་འོངས་པའི་དོན་ལ་རང་བཞིན་གྱི་སྒྲ་གྱི་བརྟན་པ
ཚེ་སྲིད་རང་བཞིན་གྱི་བརླག་རྟགས་འགྲེལ་བ
གང་འདི་སྲིད་པའི་གྲིབ་ནས་རྣམ་གྲོལ་བར་བྱེད་དགོས་པ
ཐུ་མཐའ་དཀའ་བ་ནས་ངོ་བོར་བསྟན་པ གདོང་གི་སྟོང་མའི་རང་ངོ་ལ་བསྒྱུར་བའི་ཚུལ
རང་ངོའི་ལུས་སེལ་ནས་གསལ་བ དགོན་པའི་འོད་ཟེར་འོད་གསལ་བའི་བརྟན་གྲུབ་དང་མཛེས་བ
ཡེ་ཤེས་གསལ་བ་ནས་གང་ལ་ཀྱང་དགོས་པ ཐུ་མཐའ་འགྲོ་མེད་ནས་འོད་ཟེར་གསལ་བ
ཉི་མའི་འོད་ལ་གཅིག་པར་འོངས་པ

Open the gates to true existence

Stillness, one door to everlasting space

Silence, a shining luminous presence

Discovering flaming heart felt joy is true life

Between thoughts, see the space

Glow is your eternal nature

untouched and whole.

Life vitality always prevails

Life's vitality always prevails, Dancing with luminous energy, deep in the endless sea. Walk through it, and you will find yourself, Not in searching, but in resting effortlessly.

In darkness, longing for a guiding light, Lost in confusion, struggling to see. But when wisdom arises, all becomes clear, Clarity dissolves all doubt—reality shines free.

Come back home, where your true self resides, No heaviness, no pain—the truth is here. Time fades when light is discovered, Spontaneous manifestation sparks within.

Waves of truth, waves of love, waves of compassion, In the ocean of existence, many faces, one truth. Even in the darkest night, when all hope seems lost, Emptiness reveals itself as luminous presence.

I searched for answers, yet they remained hidden, In the depths of the soul, confusion reigned supreme. But then a light appeared, shining brightly— Not found, but recognized, always present within.

དེ་དགོངས་པའི་བདེན་སྤྲུལ་གྱི་སྒྲོ་སྒྲིག ཞི་བའི་སྒྲོ་ལ་གང་ཡང་མེད་པའི་དཀའ་བ
ཞི་བ་དང་དང་དུ་སྒྲོལ་བའི་འོད་འབར་བ
དགའ་བའི་མཛེས་མོ་དང་འཁོར་བའི་ཚུལ་རིགས་ལྡན་པ
སྣ་བའི་རང་ངོ་རེ་བར་དགོས་པ་ལས་འོངས་པ
འོད་འོངས་པའི་དོན་ལ་རང་བཞིན་གྱི་སྒྲ་གྱི་བརྟན་པ
ཚེ་སྲིད་རང་བཞིན་གྱི་བརླག་རྟགས་འགྲེལ་བ
གང་འདི་སྲིད་པའི་གྲིབ་ནས་རྣམ་གྲོལ་བར་བྱེད་དགོས་པ
མུ་མཐའ་དཀའ་བ་ནས་ངོ་བོར་བསྟན་པ
གདོང་གི་སྟོང་མའི་རང་ངོ་ལ་བསྒྱུར་བའི་ཚུལ རང་ངོའི་ལུས་སེལ་ནས་གསལ་བ
དགོན་པའི་འོད་ཟེར་འོད་གསལ་བའི་བརྟན་གྲུབ་དང་མཛེས་བ
ཡེ་ཤེས་གསལ་བ་ནས་གང་ལ་ཀྱང་དགོས་པ
མུ་མཐའ་འགྲོ་མེད་ནས་འོད་ཟེར་གསལ་བ ཉེ་མའི་འོད་ལ་གཅིག་པར་འོངས་པ

སྐྱེ་མའི་སྒྲ་འཁོར་བའི་འོད་གསལ་བ་ལ་མཛེས་བ
རང་རིག་གྲོལ་བའི་སྒྲ་ཡིད་ཀྱི་གསུངས་སུ་གཟིགས་པ
གང་ནམ་དཀའ་བ་ནས་གདོན་མེད་དུ་འགྲོ་བ གདོན་མེད་སྒྲང་དུ་བརྟེན་པ
གང་ནམ་འོད་འགྲོགས་པར་འབྱུངས་པ
རང་བཞིན་ལ་འོངས་པ་དང་རང་ངོ་ལ་བཙུག་པ
སྒྲོ་བའི་གྲུབ་ཐབས་ཀྱི་འཁོར་ལས་རིག་བ
རང་ངོ་སྣང་མང་པོ་དང་འགྲོ་མེད་འོད་ཙངས་ཀྱི་མཐར་གྱི་སྒྲ

Oh, guiding star, lead me back home

Through the chaos and the unknown

Oh, wisdom's voice, whisper in my ear whisper in my ear

Bring me back to where I belong, free from fear

When lost, discover a shining light.

Confusion is dissolved as wisdom arises,

come back home, in the deeps, your self remains.

Spontaneous manifestation rises.

Waves of truth, waves of love, of joy

waves of compassion, of pace,

one ocean, many faces, one truth.

Written by Tagzig To my Master who gave me a true life.

Ocean Waves - རྒྱ་མཚོའི་འཕྱུར་འཁྲུག

In the depths of the ocean, where purity resides
རྒྱ་མཚོའི་སྨད་ཁའི་གཙང་དག་ཡིན་པར།
Luminous waves dance, with secrets they confide
འོད་གསལ་གྱི་འཕུར་འཁྲུག་གསང་བའི་སྟོན་པ།
Edges glistening, with an eternal glow
དུས་ཡུན་མེད་པའི་འོད་དང་འཁྲུག་པ།
All-pervading sunshine, through me and through you
ང་དང་ཁྱེད་རང་ནང་ཡང་འོད་དང་འཁྲུག་པ།

When the truth is lost, but never truly dies
བདེན་པ་ལེན་མི་འགོ་ལ་ཡང་མི་འཆི།
Your inner self rises, reaching for the skies
ཁྱེད་རང་གི་ནང་བཞིན་གྱི་གནས་ཚུལ་གྲོངས་ཡོད།

When my body is left behind, my essence lives on
བདག་གི་སྐུ་ལྡན་བཞིན་ཡོད་པར་རང་བཞིན་གི་བརྫོ
ད་པ།
Divine nature, everlasting, forever strong
རྣམ་པར་རྫོད་པའི་གནས་ཚུལ་རྟོགས་པ།

When lost, come back home to our indestructible essence,
བརླགས་ན་རང་བཞིན་ལ་འཇུག་གཏོང་ན།
aging does not exist when pure nature is realized.
གཙང་དག་བཞིན་དུ་ཤེས་ན་རྒ་རྩོད་མེད།

In the search for truth, we wander far and wide
བདེན་པ་འཚོལ་ན་རིགས་ཀྱི་སྣང་བ་འགྲུབ།
Underneath a sky that stretches out so wide
ནམ་མཁའ་རྒྱ་ཆེན་པའི་འདི་ནང་འདོད་དི་པ།
But when the compass fails and we lose our way
འཛིན་པ་གཏོར་ན་སྐུ་དག་པའི་རྒྱ་ཆེན་པ།
It's in our core, where we find solace and stay
གཟུགས་ཀྱི་རྟོགས་པ་ནང་གསལ་ཞིང་བཟང་པོ།

Oh, come back home to the unfading self
བསྐྱོད་མི་བརླགས་པར་སྐྱོང་ཞིང་ཡིན།
Where time stands still and love can freely help
དུས་མི་སྒོང་ན་ཉམས་མེད་པ།
Brush away the illusions that cloud your view
འཁྲུགས་འཁྲུག་དང་བཅོས་པ་གསོལ་ནི།

To my Master who gave me a true life.
ང་ལ་བདེན་པའི་སྐུ་བཞིན་གྱི་སྙིང་རྗེ་སྤྲོས་མ
ེད་མཛོད་མཁན་ལ།

Written By Tagzig

Ocean Waves : Interp

retatio

n

The poem presented, "Ocean Waves - རྒྱ་མཚོའི་འཕྱུར་འཁྲུག," offers meditation practitioners a contemplative journey through themes of purity, luminosity, truth, self-discovery, and spiritual guidance.

The poem invites an exploration of its deeper meaning through the lens of Dzogchen, a profound and direct path within Tibetan Buddhism that focuses on recognizing the ultimate nature of reality. The imagery of ocean waves, as reflected in the title, often serves as a powerful metaphor for the ceaseless arising and passing of thoughts and experiences within the vast expanse of consciousness, a central theme in Buddhist philosophy.

Line-by-Line Explanation and Commentary:

Line 1: In the depths of the ocean, where purity resides / རྒྱ་མཚོའི་སྨད་ཁའི་གཙང་དག་ཡིན་པར།

The opening line establishes a profound setting in the "depths of the ocean," a symbol often associated with the fundamental ground of being or the vastness of consciousness in various spiritual traditions. Within this deep and often unseen realm, the poem locates "purity," a concept that resonates deeply with the Dzogchen understanding of Primordial Purity, or Kadag. Kadag is described as the inherent, unconditioned purity of the nature of mind and reality itself, existing from the very beginning. This purity is not something attained or created but is the intrinsic essence of mind, free from defilements and conceptual elaborations. Just as the depths of the ocean are undisturbed by surface waves, Kadag represents the fundamental ground of being that remains pure and unstained by the fluctuations of experience. This initial focus on purity in the deepest aspect of existence immediately connects to a core Dzogchen principle, suggesting that the poem will explore the nature of our most fundamental being.

Line 2: Luminous waves dance, with secrets they confide / འོད་གསལ་གྱི་འཕྱུར་འཁྲུག་གསང་བའི་སྟོན་པ།

The imagery shifts to "luminous waves" that "dance," introducing the dynamic aspect of existence. The term "luminous" strongly connects with "Od-sal" , the Dzogchen term for luminosity or clear light, which is a key characteristic of the nature of mind and the Ground (Gzhi). This luminosity is often associated with the Sambhogakaya aspect of the Buddha and the spontaneous presence (Lhun-drub) of the Ground. The dancing of these waves suggests the ever-changing nature of appearances within this luminous expanse. Furthermore, the idea that these waves "confide secrets" hints at the inherent wisdom and potential for awakening that reside within this luminous nature. These secrets could be linked to the intrinsic potential of awareness. The dynamic and radiant quality of these waves suggests that profound understanding arises from recognizing the luminous nature of mind.

Line 3: Edges glistening, with an eternal glow / དུས་ཡུན་མེད་པའི་འོད་དང་འཁྲུག་པ།

The description of "edges glistening" could refer to the boundaries of our perceptions or experiences, illuminated by the inherent luminosity. The phrase "eternal glow" points towards something beyond the temporal, aligning with the timeless nature of the fundamental ground (Gzhi) in Dzogchen. This glow could be the unchanging radiance of Rigpa, the knowledge of the ground. The Ground (Gzhi) is described as atemporal and unchanging , and the concept of an eternal element or glow is discussed in Buddhist philosophy in relation to the ultimate, unchanging nature of reality, contrasting with the impermanence of conditioned phenomena. This line emphasizes the enduring quality of the fundamental reality that underlies our fleeting experiences.

Line 4: All-pervading sunshine, through me and through you / ང་དང་ཁྱེད་རང་ནང་ཡང་འོད་དང་འཁྱུག་པ།

The image of "all-pervading sunshine" serves as a powerful metaphor for light and awareness that is universally present. In Dzogchen, Rigpa, or pure awareness, is understood to be present in all sentient beings. The phrase "through me and through you" emphasizes the interconnectedness of all beings and the shared nature of this all-pervading awareness. Just as sunshine permeates everything, this intrinsic awareness is not separate but is the fundamental nature shared by all. The all-pervading nature of sunshine can be seen as analogous to the all-pervading nature of the divine or ultimate reality. This line highlights the universal and interconnected nature of the luminous awareness, emphasizing that it is not confined to the individual but is the very fabric of existence.

Line 5: When the truth is lost, but never truly dies / བདེན་པ་ཤེན་མི་འགོལ་ཡང་མི་འཆི།

This line speaks to a fundamental truth that can become obscured from our immediate awareness, often due to ignorance (Ma-rigpa) , but which inherently remains and cannot be destroyed. This aligns with the Dzogchen understanding of the ever-present nature of Buddha-nature or Rigpa, which is primordially pure and free from limitations, even when veiled by delusion. Even when we fail to recognize it, this essential truth of our being persists.

Line 6: Your inner self rises, reaching for the skies / ཁྱེད་རང་གི་ནང་བཞིན་གྱི་གནས་ཚུལ་གྲོངས་ཡོད།

The image of "your inner self rises, reaching for the skies" suggests an inherent potential within each individual to awaken to their true nature (Rigpa) or to aspire towards enlightenment. This rising can be seen in the context of Direct Introduction (Ngo-tro), which aims to awaken the intrinsic nature of mind. The act of reaching for the skies symbolizes a yearning to transcend current limitations and connect with a higher reality.

Line 7: When my body is left behind, my essence lives on / བདག་གི་སྐུ་ལྷན་བཞིན་ཡོད་པར་རང་བཞིན་གི་བརྗོད་པ།

This line addresses the impermanent nature of the physical body and the continuity of essence or consciousness beyond death, a central theme in Buddhist philosophy. While Dzogchen emphasizes recognizing the present nature of mind, the implication here aligns with the broader Buddhist understanding that something continues after the dissolution of the physical form, although not a permanent, unchanging self. In Dzogchen, this could relate to the recognition of Rigpa as the ground that transcends the physical body, potentially leading to advanced practices like Tögal and the realization of the rainbow body.

Line 8: Divine nature, everlasting, forever strong / རྣམ་པར་རྗོད་པའི་གནས་ཚུལ་རྟོགས་པ།

The phrase "divine nature, everlasting, forever strong" points to the inherent perfection and enduring quality of our true nature, often referred to as Buddha-nature or Rigpa in Dzogchen. Dzogchen posits that this Buddha-nature is intrinsic to all beings, perfect and unchanging from the very beginning. This line affirms the inherent potential for enlightenment within everyone, characterized by its timeless and powerful essence.

Line 9: When lost, come back home to our indestructible essence, / བརྣགས་ན་རང་བཞིན་ལ་འཇུག་གཏོང་ན།

This line serves as a direct call to return to our fundamental, unchanging nature (Rigpa or Sem-nyid) when feeling lost or disconnected from our true selves. Dzogchen emphasizes the importance of recognizing our ground and resting in our true nature. The concept of an "indestructible essence" aligns with the inherent perfection and unchanging quality of Rigpa, which Direct Introduction aims to reveal.

Line 10: aging does not exist when pure nature is realized. / གཙང་དག་བཞིན་དུ་ཤེས་ན་རྒ་རྒོད་མེད།

This line suggests that the realization of our pure nature (Rigpa), particularly its primordial purity (Kadag), transcends the limitations of time and the process of aging. The realized state in Dzogchen is often described as being beyond conceptual time and the cycle of Samsara, which includes birth, aging, sickness, and death. This reflects the Dzogchen understanding of a state beyond conceptual limitations and effort.

Line 11: In the search for truth, we wander far and wide / བདེན་པ་འཚོལ་ན་རིགས་ཀྱི་སྣང་བ་འཕྲུག།

This line acknowledges the common human experience of seeking truth and the often circuitous and challenging nature of the spiritual journey. It speaks to the external and internal explorations we undertake in our quest for understanding and meaning.

Line 12: Underneath a sky that stretches out so wide

/ ནམ་མཁའ་རྣ་ཆེན་པའི་འདི་ནང་འདོད་པ།

The imagery of a "sky that stretches out so wide" often symbolizes the vastness of emptiness, the boundless nature of mind (Sem-nyid), or the expanse of reality (Dharmadhatu) in Dzogchen. Just as the sky encompasses all, the nature of mind is described as empty, spacious, and pure, providing the ground for all phenomena to arise.

Line 13: But when the compass fails and we lose our way / འཛིན་པ་གཏོར་ན་སྣ་དག་པའི་རྣ་ཆེན་པ།

This line speaks to the limitations of relying solely on conventional means of guidance, whether external teachings or internal conceptual frameworks, in the search for ultimate truth. When these fail, we may feel lost on our spiritual path.

Line 14: It's in our core, where we find solace and stay / གཞུགས་ཀྱི་རྟོགས་པ་ནང་གསལ་ཞིང་བཟང་པོ།

The phrase "in our core" points to the inherent nature of mind, the Buddha-nature or Rigpa that resides within each being. It suggests that true and lasting peace and stability are found not externally but by turning inward and recognizing our own fundamental being, which is the aim of Direct Introduction in Dzogchen.

Line 15: Oh, come back home to the unfading self /

བསྒྲོད་མི་བརླགས་པར་སྒྲོང་ཞིང་ཡིན།

This is a repeated and direct call to return to our true self (Rigpa), which is described as "unfading," suggesting something beyond change and impermanence. This aligns with the Dzogchen emphasis on recognizing and abiding in our true nature, which is always present and does not fade away. This also relates to the concept of returning to the effortless, natural state of being.

Line 16: Where time stands still and love can freely help / དུས་མི་སྒྲོང་ན་ཉམས་མེད་པ།

This line describes the nature of the realized state as one where the conventional experience of time ceases, and love, likely referring to compassion (Thugs-rje) in a Buddhist context, arises spontaneously and acts as a guiding force. This timeless state and the spontaneous arising of compassion are characteristic of the Dzogchen understanding of ultimate reality. The timelessness also connects to the concept of Effortless Being.

Line 17: Brush away the illusions that cloud your view / འཁྲུགས་འཁྲུག་དང་བཙོས་པ་གསོལ་ཞི།

This line directly relates to the Dzogchen practice of cutting through illusions and recognizing the true nature of reality. This aligns with the practices of Trekchö and Self-Liberation (Rang-grol) , which involve actively dispelling distorted perceptions and allowing thoughts and emotions to liberate themselves.

Line 18: To my Master who gave me a true life. /

ང་ལ་བདེན་པའི་སྣ་བཞིན་གྱི་སྙིང་རྗེ་སྟོབས་མེད་མཛད་མཁན་ལ།

The final line expresses profound gratitude towards a spiritual teacher or Master, highlighting the crucial role of the Guru in guiding practitioners on the Dzogchen path to the realization of their true nature. The Direct Introduction (Ngo-tro) to Rigpa is typically bestowed by a qualified Master, leading to a genuine understanding or experience of reality, which the speaker gratefully acknowledges as a "true life."

Overall Themes and Dzogchen Interpretation:

The poem "Ocean Waves" intricately weaves together core themes that deeply resonate with Dzogchen philosophy. The inherent purity and luminosity of existence are introduced in the opening lines, aligning with the Dzogchen concepts of Kadag and Od-sal. The poem then explores the obscuration of this fundamental truth by illusion, a state of ignorance (Ma-rigpa) that prevents the recognition of our true nature (Rigpa). The journey of seeking truth, often fraught with wandering and the failure of conventional guidance, is acknowledged, emphasizing the importance of turning inward to our own core nature, our Buddha-nature, to find lasting peace and solace.

The poem repeatedly calls us back to this "unfading self," a direct pointer to recognizing Rigpa, our pure and timeless awareness. The realized state is depicted as one where the limitations of time cease to hold sway, and compassion (Thugs-rje) arises spontaneously, guiding our actions. The imperative to "brush away the illusions" directly reflects the Dzogchen practice of Trekchö, cutting through delusion to reveal the primordially pure nature of mind. Finally, the expression of gratitude towards the Master underscores the indispensable role of lineage and direct transmission in the Dzogchen path.

The poem, therefore, can be seen as a concise and poetic expression of the Dzogchen view and path. It gently guides the reader towards the recognition of their own inherent perfection, emphasizing the ever-present potential for awakening that lies within, obscured only by the temporary clouds of illusion. The journey described mirrors the essence of Dzogchen: a direct path to realizing the already enlightened state of our own mind.

Conclusion:

In conclusion, the poem "Ocean Waves - རྒྱ་མཚོའི་འཕྱུར་འཁྲུག།" offers a profound contemplative reflection that aligns remarkably well with the core tenets of Dzogchen Buddhism. Through its evocative imagery of the ocean, waves, sunshine, and sky, the poem explores themes of inherent purity and luminosity, the journey of self-discovery, the transcendence of limitations, and the crucial role of spiritual guidance. The line-by-line analysis reveals strong connections to key Dzogchen concepts such as Kadag, Od-sal, Lhun-drub, Rigpa, and the significance of the Guru. The poem serves as a powerful reminder of our intrinsic enlightened nature and the potential for realizing this truth through introspection and the dispelling of illusions, ultimately leading us back "home" to our unfading self.

Meditation Practices

9 Breaths Exercise

Pranajana or breath control, also works as shamata, mind training. With the exercise of the 9 breaths you work with prana or vital energy, which is closely related to your mind.

First, think about something in your life that makes you angry, then about something else that you feel desire for, then about something that you feel doubt about or lack of clarity; these are the dripa (mental obscurations); relate to né (illness) or to the dön (emotional obstacle).

Chánels:

- **Right Channel on the right side**: is masculine energy, negative emotions, method channel, lunar energy, associated with clarity. It measures approximately one centimeter in diameter and goes from the lower abdomen to the right nostril.

- The Red Channel on the left side: is feminine energy, positive emotions, channel of wisdom, solar energy, associated with em. It measures approximately one centimeter in diameter and goes from the lower abdomen to the left nostril.

- The blue Channel in the center: it is the channel of Non-duality, energy of RIGPA or awakened Consciousness. It is about the thickness of a thumb, starting in the lower abdomen and ascending in a straight line until it opens at the crown of the head.

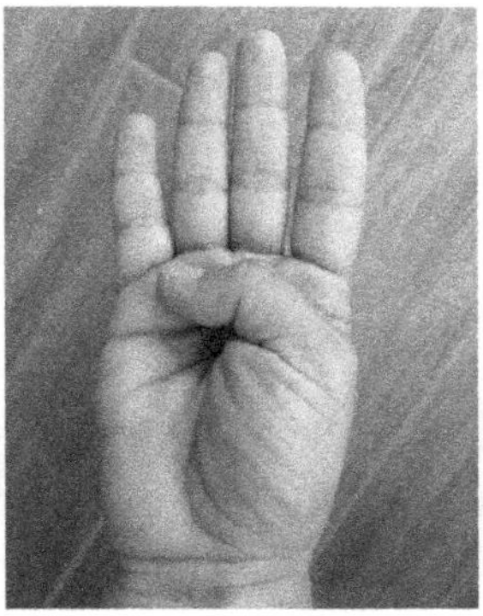

Visualize the three channels, now with the right hand, close the right nostril, relate to the anger, its images, deeper and deeper.

1. **PURIFY ANGER** _Purify sadness, hate, pride, anger, dislike or the obstacles of the past. Inhale through the left nostril, covering the right nostril with your thumb;

Visualize as the WHITE CHANNEL enters the air that enters the vital energy (prana) of green color of healing, which goes down through the RED CHANNEL on the left side of the body, in

So much does emotion take to purify; Visualize that the energy, now blue in color, exits through the RED CHANNEL on the left side of the body, dragging with it the emotion to be purified. Forcefully expels the air through the right nostril, as if the emotion to be purified was "squeezed" with it as you contract your diaphragm, exhaling the diseases associated with wind and obstacles. Feel the quality of space in the breath. Relate to the levels of image, energy and space. REPEAT 3 TIMES.

2. **PURIFY ATTACHMENT**

Also the clinging, the desire, the jealousy, the obstacles of the present.

Relate to your attachment or desire, to its images, or to being stuck in those feelings. Think of purifying this at the level of body, energy and mind with each breath you take;

Inhale through the right nostril, the energy enters through the RED CHANNEL, covering the left nostril with the thumb; feel how the green energy enters, which enters together with the air and that goes down through the **WHITE CHANNEL** on the right side of your body and purifies diseases associated with Bile, mental obscurations associated with attachment and purification of Future Karma.

Forcefully expel the air through the left nostril and with it comes out pink lung. Feel the quality of space, releasing obstacles and affirm that the space is now full of vital and divine energy. REPEAT x 3 TIMES.

3. **PURIFY DOUBT**

Ignorance or lack of clarity generates disconnection from your true nature, lack of confidence and fears, the obstacles that you have created for yourself in the present.

Put equanimity in your hands. Visualize the CENTRAL BLUE CHANNEL, the channel of Non-duality. Relate to ignorance, to diseases associated with phlegm;

Visualize how a green light enters through both nostrils with the air and in a cascade of energy runs through BOTH SIDE CHANNELS of your body, while it takes the emotion to purify, it enters through both side channels until it reaches the base where the green energy it unites with the CENTRAL CHANNEL of blue color and thus all the mental obscurations associated with ignorance come out, purifying the Karma of the present. Exits through both nostrils exhaling slowly.

As you exhale, feel as if the energy were coming out of the top of your head, expelling it in a deep smoky color. You contract the diaphragm, which helps you expel the energy through your head;Feel all Rigpa experience that is your pure essence, it is the union between infinite space (divine nature omnipresent) (divine nature is omniscient) and clear light, the awakened consciousness, which takes place in the central channel. REPEAT 3 TIMES.

Guru Yoga Meditation:

This meditation begins with a sacred sound and connects you with the light and blessings of all enlightened beings.

Assume a comfortable and stable position. Sit with your back straight but relaxed, whether in full lotus, half lotus, or kneeling on a cushion. If you prefer a chair, ensure your feet are firmly on the ground. Gently close your eyes or keep them softly open with a defocused gaze. Allow your hands to rest comfortably in your lap or on your knees.

The teachings of Tapihritsa embody Dzogchen's essence. From his appearance in pure light to his transmission of the highest wisdom, his message remains: **Liberation is effortless, available now, beyond striving, beyond illusion.**

Invocation and Reception of Divine Light

At this moment, raise your intention. Feel the presence of beings of light, enlightened masters, or the divine energy that resonates with you—whether it's Buddha, Jesus, or any other being of pure compassion and wisdom. Sense a **Ray of Divine Light** descending towards you from above, a stream of pure energy and blessings.

Now, with this intention, softly and prolongedly pronounce the syllable "A" (Ahhh). As you vocalize "A," feel this ray of light entering through the crown of your head, at your Crown Chakra. Visualize or feel this light flooding your head, expanding, filling you with profound peace and crystalline clarity. Feel the blessings of the universe and all accompanying beings of light.

Conscious Breathing and Heart Expansion

Direct your attention to your breath, and now, inhale twice as much as you normally would. Pronounce the syllable "A" (Ahhh). Take a deep, conscious breath, drawing the air deep into your abdomen, allowing your chest to expand completely.

With each long, slow exhalation, release any tension, worry, or attachment. Feel it dissolve and leave you. With each deep, prolonged inhalation, breathe in and fill yourself with joy, light, love, and everything you need right now. Feel these divine qualities nourish you from within.

Continue this conscious breathing, allowing the light from the Crown Chakra to descend through your central energetic channel to the center of your chest, in your Heart Chakra. Here, visualize or feel the light condense and form a radiant, luminous sphere. This sphere is your **Full Being**, the ardent clarity of your own consciousness. Feel this sphere of light forming and beginning to radiate, filling your heart with warmth and immense peace.

Channel Irradiation and Dissolution of Being

Keep your attention on the sphere of light in your heart and continue to prolong the syllable "A." Now, feel how the light from this sphere not only radiates within your heart but expands into your three main energy channels: the central channel and the two side channels (one to the left and one to the right of your spinal column).

Visualize or feel this brilliant light filling these three channels, and from them, extending to all your chakras, illuminating, purifying, and balancing them one by one. Feel the energy flowing freely throughout your entire being.

Continue to prolong the syllable "A," allowing the sphere of light in your heart to expand further. Now, visualize or feel this light extending beyond your main channels to all your sub-energetic channels, branching out like a **tree of light** throughout your entire body, filling every cell, every tissue, every fiber of your being with its radiance. Your entire energetic body becomes illuminated.

Finally, as the syllable "A" resonates within you, allow the sphere of light in your heart to expand even more, radiating with such intensity that your physical body—your sense of ego, of limited individuality—begins to dissolve into this light. Feel your form merge with the infinite, luminous space surrounding you, without limits, without boundaries.

Remain in this sensation of vast, boundless unity. You are the **lamp before the cave**, the **spark before the fire rains**. You are the song that sings the singer, the voice of silence, subtle and constant. You are like the **blue sky**: untouched, spotless, needing no support. You are the **mirror that holds fire without burning**, the **water that flows without form**, giving everything without losing itself.

Rest in this pure and serene consciousness, which waits eternally, judges not, nor condemns. Always present. When you feel ready to return, inhale deeply, feel your body's presence, and gently open your eyes, bringing with you the calm and light you've cultivated within.

✧ Dedication Prayer ✧

In the Light of Dzogchen, May all beings swiftly awaken to their true nature. May we abide, in life and beyond, in the open expanse of the mind's pure essence. Unborn, unceasing — clear, luminous, and free. May the moment of death be a door to timeless presence. And may boundless compassion embrace all worlds.

21 Semzins: Dzogchen Methods for Settling Mind and Realizing Reality

The Semzins are specialized Dzogchen[2] meditation techniques aimed at stabilizing presence, cutting through mental fixation, and deepening direct recognition of reality beyond conceptual grasping. Below are several profound Semzin practices, refined for clarity and accessibility. The practices designed to introduce, stabilize, and deepen recognition of the natural state (Rigpa). The term Semzin (སེམས་འཛིན་) means "holding the mind" or "fixation of mind", but in Dzogchen, these are not rigid concentration exercises.

---

[2] Garab Dorje & Shri Singha: ➡ Laid the foundation for direct recognition, aligning Semzin methods with spontaneous realization.
Longchenpa & Jigme Lingpa: ➡ Integrated Semzin practices into a holistic system, emphasizing effortless presence and natural perfection.

Instead, they are skillful methods for relaxing, clarifying, and integrating the mind, body, and senses, ultimately leading to direct experience of nondual awareness.

Traditionally, these practices are grouped into **three series**:

A. Calming and Settling the Mind

B. Overcoming Attachment to Body and Mind

C. Understanding the True Nature of Existence

Refuge & Compa

ssion

Prayer

Enlightened beings, beings of light

Here me now my only desire

Illumination for the freedom of all beings

Beings of light

In this life:

I am peace

I am joy

I am love

Compasión Perfect and puré arise naturally.

A crystal lotus, Shining in me.

Ah, Ah Ah: I live in Light.

བོད་ཀྱི་དཀྱིལ་འཁོར། བོད་ཟེར་གྱི་མཁར།
འཛིག་རྟེན་གང་ཡང་ངའི་ནང་ལ་ཡོད།
ཐམས་ཅད་ནང་ཡོད་པས། མཐའ་ཡས་སྣང་བ། མཉམ་པ་རེད།

བོད་ཟེར་གྱི་དབྱིངས་ལས། རིགས་ཀུན་གནས་པ།
གསུང་བ་ཉམས་སུ་བཞུགས་པའི་གནས་དག་པ། ཐུགས་རྗེ་ཆེ།

མཐའ་ཡས་དགའ་བ།
རང་ཡིན་པ་ཡང་ན། བསྐྱར་མེད་དུ་ཡོད།

Manda
la

Prayer

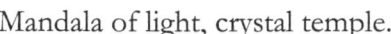

Mandala of light, crystal temple.

The universe inside of me.

All is within, boundless view, all is equal.

Facets of Light, eternal goodness.

Abiding in sacred space. Thanks

Infinite joy,

just to be, just to be..

A. The First Series: Calming and Settling the Mind

General Principle:

Let the **mind and body relax completely**. Release all **effort, judgment, and conceptualization**. The **goal** is to rest in **effortless presence**, allowing **calm and clarity** to arise naturally.

1. White "A" on the Tip of the Nose

- **Method:** Visualize a luminous white **"A"** at the tip of your **nose**, moving **with the breath.**
- **Comment:** Combines **gentle concentration with breath awareness**, anchoring the mind and **calming discursive thought**. The **"A"** symbolizes **primordial purity** in Dzogchen.

2. Relaxed Fixation and the PHAT!

- **Method:** After **relaxing fixation**, allow thoughts to **arise**, then sharply **shout "PHAT!"**, and **rest in the resulting state.**
- **Comment: "PHAT!"** is a classic Dzogchen technique for **cutting through discursive mind** and **directly accessing clarity and emptiness.**

3. The Laughter of Wrathful and Joyous Manifestations ("HA")

- **Method:** Sound **"HA"** loudly and quickly **in a state of presence.**
- **Comment:** Sound invokes **clarity and cuts through subtle distractions.**

4. The Struggle of the Asuras

- **Method:** Sit **hugging knees**, roll **head slowly** with eyes **closed**.
- **Comment:** This **somatic technique** massages the **neck and nervous system**, helping thoughts **subside** while presence remains.

5. Sounding "HUNG"

- **Method:** Sound **"HUNG"** slowly and deeply, **maintaining relaxed attention**.
- **Comment: "HUNG"** is the seed syllable of **the indestructible nature of mind**.

6. Visualizing "RAM" at the Navel Chakra

- **Method:** Visualize and sound **"RAM"** at the **navel**, integrating **breath and sensation**.
- **Comment:** Awakens **bodily presence**, grounding awareness in **the fire element**.

7. Deity Visualization at the Nose

- **Method:** Visualize a **deity at the tip of the nose**, moving with the **breath**, then imagine infinite forms **emanating and returning**.
- **Comment:** Leads to **clarity and purity**, combining **breath, visualization, and presence**.

B. The Second Series: Overcoming Attachment to Body and Mind

General Principle:

These practices **transcend fixation** on **body and subtle energies**, leading to **non-attachment** and **energetic balance**.

8. Pink Sphere Between the Eyebrows

- **Method:** Visualize a **pink sphere**, representing the **union of lunar and solar energies.**
- **Comment:** Balances **subtle energies**, inducing **visions or sensations.**

9. Central and Side Channel Visualization

- **Method:** Visualize the **central channel expanding and contracting**, then the **side channels**, integrating **breath and visualization.**
- **Comment:** Clears **energetic blockages**, harmonizing **prana (life force).**

10. White Ball on the Nose

- **Method:** Visualize a **white ball** moving with the **breath**, traveling to **distant lands.**
- **Comment:** Uses **breath awareness** as a **vehicle for presence.**

C. The Third Series: Understanding the True Nature of Existence

General Principle:

These semzins foster **direct realization** of **emptiness, impermanence, and nonduality.**

15. Gradual Understanding of Emptiness, or Space

- **Method:** Analyze the **body and environment** down to **atoms**, discovering the **absence of inherent essence.**
- **Comment:** Leads to **insight into emptiness**, beyond **intellectual understanding.**

16. Direct Understanding of Emptiness

- **Method:** Remain **present with appearances**, without **judgment or analysis.**
- **Comment:** Moves beyond **conceptual grasping**, into **pure non-conceptual experience.**

17. The Semzin of Impermanence

- **Principle:** Everything is impermanent—moving, shifting, and dissolving. Manifestation is unreal, transient, and beyond judgment.
- **Practice:** Be present in **the continuous change of reality** without conceptual interference. Let go of **definitions and mental reification**—things arise and dissolve without fixed existence.
- **Effect:** This leads to a **state beyond concepts**, where one feels **at the center of the experience yet unattached** to identity or belonging.

◆ **Analogy:** Thoughts and perceptions are like **waves in an ocean**—they arise and dissolve, yet the ocean remains.

18. Relaxing in the Five Elements

- **Principle:** The **five elements** (earth, water, fire, air, space) define all experience. Instead of fixating on them, simply **relax into their presence without distraction.**
- **Practice:** Upon encountering an element (such as wind touching the skin or sunlight warming the body), **recognize its presence immediately** without conceptual processing. Let experience remain **pure and raw.**
- **Effect:** This practice enhances **non-attachment,** fostering a sensation **similar to lucid dreaming**, where everything is vivid yet insubstantial.

◆ **Key Insight:** Experience **the element directly without elaboration**, allowing presence to absorb its raw qualities.

19. Presence in the Instant After a Thought Arises

- **Principle:** Thoughts arise and dissolve rapidly, creating the **illusion of continuity**. Presence halts this timeline, revealing the **gap beyond mental constructions**.
- **Practice:** When a thought arises, **pause immediately** and remain in its **after-state** without following its conceptual trail. Apply the same principle to **sensory impressions**—see something, but remain **free from mental labeling**.
- **Effect:** This creates **"thought-free presence"**, breaking the illusion that thoughts are inherently solid.

◆ **Analogy:** The **raw moment** is like uncooked grain—it remains pure. **Thought cooks the raw moment into conceptual solidity**. Stay present in the **naked moment before conceptual processing**.

20. The Semzin of Union

- **Principle:** Experience the **clarity of manifestation before mental activity** distorts perception. Presence in this **pre-conceptual state** leads to **self-liberated experience**.
- **Practice:** As soon as an object appears before the senses, **remain in presence before interpretation begins**. In deep contemplation, this state unveils **non-duality**, where perception exists without a subject-object divide.
- **Effect:** This enhances clarity and immediate awareness, making all phenomena self-liberating and effortless.

◆ **Union in Sensation:** Physical sensations—including **pleasure and touch**—can be used to recognize **emptiness beyond conceptualization**.

21. The Semzin of Space and Integration

- **Principle:** All phenomena share the **same nature as space**—luminous yet empty, present yet unsupported.
- **Practice:** Visualize a **HUNG syllable or sphere traveling through space**, dissolving limitations and revealing the **infinitude of experience.** Let **all mental activity merge into vast spaciousness.**
- **Effect:** A complete **integration into contemplation**, where experience becomes **inseparable from space itself**—boundless, non-fixed, effortless.

◆ **Key Insight:** Let **all mental grasping dissolve into space**, recognizing that **nothing requires external support to exist.**

The **21 Semzins** provide an **effortless path** to stabilizing **Rigpa**, dissolving **mental constructs**, and resting in **spontaneous presence.** Whether used as **formal practice or integrated into daily life**, they remain **timeless, transformative, and accessible** to anyone seeking **awakening beyond conceptual fixation.**

The **Ten Perfections (Pāramitās)** in Buddhism, known in Tibetan as *par chen chu* (ཕར་ཆེན་བཅུ་), represent virtues that lead to enlightenment. These qualities are cultivated by Bodhisattvas on their path to Buddhahood:

- **Dāna Pāramitā** – Generosity: The practice of selfless giving and kindness.
- **Śīla Pāramitā** – Morality: Ethical conduct, discipline, and integrity.
- **Nekkhamma Pāramitā** – Renunciation: Letting go of attachments and desires.
- **Prajñā Pāramitā** – Wisdom: Insight into the true nature of reality.
- **Vīrya Pāramitā** – Energy: Diligence, perseverance, and effort in spiritual practice.
- **Kṣānti Pāramitā** – Patience: Endurance, tolerance, and acceptance.
- **Satyā Pāramitā** – Truthfulness: Honesty and sincerity in thought, speech, and action.
- **Adhiṣṭhāna Pāramitā** – Determination: Strong resolve and unwavering commitment.
- **Maitrī Pāramitā** – Loving-kindness: Compassion and unconditional love for all beings.
- **Upekṣā Pāramitā** – Equanimity: Balanced mind, serenity, and impartiality.

These virtues are essential for spiritual progress and are emphasized in Mahāyāna Buddhism, particularly in the Bodhisattva path.

Compassion

In Dzogchen, compassion (*thugs rje*) is not merely an ethical principle or an emotional response—it is an intrinsic manifestation of the awakened mind. Unlike conventional interpretations of compassion, which often emphasize empathy and altruistic action, Dzogchen views compassion as the spontaneous radiance of primordial awareness (*rigpa*). It is inseparable from wisdom and arises naturally when one recognizes the true nature of reality.

Manifestation of Compassion in Dzogchen

1. **Spontaneous Presence** – In Dzogchen, compassion is not cultivated through effort but arises effortlessly when one abides in the natural state of awareness. It is the luminous expression of the mind's innate clarity.
2. **Beyond Duality** – Unlike conventional compassion, which may involve a subject helping an object, Dzogchen compassion transcends dualistic distinctions. It is an all-pervasive responsiveness to the suffering of beings without attachment or conceptualization.
3. **The Eight Sparks of Compassion** – Dzogchen teachings describe compassion as manifesting in various forms, such as wisdom, guidance, and direct realization. These manifestations serve as pathways for beings to awaken.
4. **Integration with Bodhicitta** – Dzogchen recognizes both relative and absolute *bodhicitta* (the mind of enlightenment). Relative *bodhicitta* involves intentional acts of kindness, while absolute *bodhicitta* is the direct realization of emptiness and interconnectedness.
5. **Compassion as the Function of Awareness** – In Dzogchen, compassion is not separate from wisdom. It is the natural function of awakened awareness, responding

fluidly to the needs of beings without conceptual interference.

Why is Compassion Important in Dzogchen?

- **Path to Liberation** – Compassion ensures that realization is not self-centered but directed toward the benefit of all beings. It prevents spiritual practice from becoming an isolated pursuit.
- **Expression of Rigpa** – True realization in Dzogchen is not passive; it radiates as compassionate activity, guiding others toward awakening.
- **Harmonization of Wisdom and Love** – Dzogchen teaches that wisdom without compassion is incomplete. Compassion ensures that realization is embodied in action, making enlightenment meaningful.
- **Dissolution of Ego** – By recognizing suffering as an illusion and responding with compassion, practitioners dissolve self-clinging and deepen their realization of emptiness.

Dzogchen's approach to compassion is profound—it is not something one must force or cultivate artificially. Instead, it is the natural radiance of an awakened mind, effortlessly benefiting all beings.

Tögal (ཐོད་རྒལ་)

Direct Crossing into Spontaneous Presence

Tögal means "crossing the abyss" and refers to advanced visualization practices and working with the natural light of the mind. This practice stabilizes the experience of *rigpa* or awakened awareness, dissolving dualistic appearances.

Tögal is also transalted as "direct crossing" or "leap-over." While Trekchö cuts through obscurations to reveal the empty essence of awareness, Tögal reveals its *luminous display.* It is the visionary practice that reveals the dynamic energy of awareness as light, forms, and mandalas.

By emphasizing that recognizing the true nature of reality and ourselves, everything is already perfect as it is. His teachings reinforce the idea that there is no need to fix, change, or judge this natural state. The true nature of mind, or rigpa, is like a vast, clear sky—open, spacious, and unaffected by the clouds that temporarily obscure it. This perspective is deeply aligned with the essence of Pure Being found in other mystical traditions, such as Advaita Vedanta and Taoism.

In Advaita Vedanta, the realization of Brahman, the ultimate reality, is similarly about recognizing the inherent perfection and unity of all existence. Taoism's principle of wu wei, or effortless action, echoes Dzogchen's teaching of resting in the natural state without effort. These traditions collectively highlight the transcendence of dualities and the realization of an ultimate, non-dual state of being, where the inner light or divine essence is recognized as already perfect and complete.

By embracing these teachings, we can move beyond the limitations of the ego and experience the boundless nature of our true being. This philosophical and mystical insight unites these spiritual paths, emphasizing the reverence for the inner journey toward ultimate reality and the profound interconnectedness of all existence.

Tenzin Wangyal Rinpoche:

"Tögal shows us that the display of light and visions is not separate from the empty, pure base. Realization is the unity of openness and spontaneous presence."

Tögal is practiced after one has stabilized in the View through Trekchö. It involves precise physical postures, gazes (such as sky-gazing), and subtle breath awareness. In dark retreats or open sky meditation, spontaneous visions of light, deities, and luminous shapes may arise.

Tögal literally means "leaping over the skull" or "direct transcendence." It is often translated as *direct vision*, *spontaneous transcendence*, or *leap-over practice*. This advanced meditative path activates the **natural light of the mind** through specific techniques, such as:

- Gazing at clear open sky
- Meditation in total darkness
- Working with subtle channels (*tsa*), inner winds (*lung*), and luminous essences (*thigle*)

These methods allow the practitioner to perceive **spontaneous luminous visions**—rainbow circles, mandalas, divine forms—which are not hallucinations, but **manifestations of the innate clarity of the mind**.

- It is practiced only after *Trekchö* is stable, as it involves **working with the subtle energetic and visionary dimensions** of rigpa.
- Techniques include:
    - **Sky-gazing**
    - **Dark retreat**
    - **Opening the channels (tsa), winds (lung), and luminous drops (thigle)**

These practices give rise to **spontaneous visionary experiences**, such as **luminous circles, rainbow mandalas, and deity forms**, unfolding through the **Four Visions of Tögal**, culminating—potentially—in the dissolution of the body into light, known as the **rainbow body (jalü)**.

> “Trekchö is wisdom. Tögal is the method.” > One reveals; the other unfolds.

☐ A-khrid Dzogchen – The Guided Path

The following translation and coments come from the original Tibetan author of the **A-khrid** [3]**Dzogchen** system is **Me’u Gongdzö (Tibetan: མེའུ་དགོངས་མཛོད་, Me’u dGongs-mdzod)**, who lived in the 11th century (circa 1038–1096). He is credited with systematizing the A-khrid (*A-tri*) teachings, which are one of the three principal Dzogchen lineages in the Bön tradition.

Later, the system was further elaborated and transmitted by **Bru-sgom rGyal-ba g.Yung-drung** (1242–1290), who composed key root texts and practice manuals that are still studied today.

So, Me’u Gongdzö is the originator, and Bru-sgom Gyalwa Yungdrung is the great codifier and transmitter of the A-khrid lineage. Let me know if you'd like a timeline or lineage chart of the A-khrid masters. ⍰

- A-khrid (ཨ་མཁྲིད་, *A-tri*) means “Guidance through the letter A,” which symbolizes **primordial emptiness** in Bön.
- Developed by **Me’u Gongdzö** in the 11th century and systematized by **Bru-sgom Gyalwa Yungdrung** in the

---

[3] **Bru-sgom rGyal-ba g.yung-drung** (1242–1290) *The Stages of A-khrid Meditation* Translated by Per Kværne & Thupten K. Rikey Published by the Library of Tibetan Works and Archives, 1996 Read the full text (PDF)
Jean-Luc Achard *Bonpo Dzogchen Teachings and the A-khrid System* Featured in various academic journals and monographs. (Searchable via Academia.edu and Oxford Research Encyclopedia)

13th, A-khrid is a **structured, step-by-step Dzogchen curriculum** within the Bön tradition.

It includes:

1. **Ngöndro** – Preliminaries: purification, refuge, mandala offerings, guru devotion
2. **Guru Yoga and Visualization** – Opening the heart to lineage blessings
3. **Direct Introduction (Ngo-sprod)** – The master points out rigpa
4. **Stabilizing the View through meditation** – Gradually deepening awareness across 80 stages or sessions

Unlike Trekchö or Tögal, which lean toward experiential immediacy, **A-khrid provides a graduated pathway**, suitable for practitioners needing structure while still aiming for the same realization of rigpa.

The Radiant Vision of Tögal in the Atri Dzogchen Tradition ✧

Tögal (*thod rgal*), often translated as "direct crossing" or "leap over," is one of the two principal practices in **Dzogchen**, alongside **Trekchö** ("cutting through"). While **Trekchö** dissolves all fixations through the naked vision of the mind as lucid emptiness, **Tögal** focuses on the luminous manifestation of the mind — the spontaneous display of pure awareness as it arises in appearances.

This text subtly presents this sublime practice through the lens of **Atri** (*A-khrid*), a progressive path of Dzogchen meditation from the **Bön tradition** that emphasizes clarity, accessibility, and systematic instruction.

✦ 1. The End of Conceptual Effort

A-khrid:

> "Thus comes the end of intellectual striving over what must be rejected."

The Tögal path does not involve rejecting thoughts or emotions. Unlike other systems that apply antidotes — for example, cultivating love to counteract anger — Tögal teaches us to **directly recognize the luminous nature** of whatever arises.

There is no longer a struggle against what appears; rather, all appearances are seen as already liberated. The concept of "using antidotes" is transcended through the immediate recognition of the mind's innate clarity and emptiness.

✦ 2. The Ocean and Sky Metaphor

A-khrid:

> "When the vast ocean is still, the waves naturally calm…"

Poetic metaphors such as the ocean, the sky, and the mind point to the essential nature of spirit: **clear, vast, serene, and beyond birth or cessation**. When we cease interference, appearances self-liberate. Just as the ocean effortlessly reflects the sky, the mind reflects thoughts without grasping at them.

✦ 3. The Three Types of Practitioners

A-khrid

The text distinguishes three levels of practitioners:

- **Superior practitioners** recognize the nature of the mind the moment an appearance arises — like **snow melting upon contact with water**: instantly dissolved, avoiding entanglement in illusion.

- **Intermediate practitioners** recognize it once appearances have arisen — like **frost vanishing under sunlight**: gently dissolving in the warmth of awareness.

- **Beginners**, even if not immediately recognizing, refrain from being swept away by afflictive passions — like one who reasons with a man chasing them in anger: not reacting blindly but holding steady.

This classification, drawn from **Atri**, presents a gradual yet direct approach. In Tögal, the aim is not to "stop" thoughts but to **see their essence from the outset**.

✦ 4. Not One-by-One, but at the Root

A-khrid

Rather than applying remedies to each thought (like pulling weeds one at a time), Tögal teaches that **recognizing the nonexistence of a separate self** is like a medicine that cures a hundred illnesses at once. This recognition is **non-conceptual** — direct, like seeing the sun with your own eyes.

✦ 5. Manifestation as Wisdom

A-khrid:

> "Eventually, all that arises will emerge as wisdom."

> "Discursive thoughts gradually subside,
> While wisdom begins to shine ever more brightly."

Tögal regards **all appearances** — lights, visions, thoughts, phenomena — as **manifestations of wisdom**. There is no separation between what arises and the awareness that knows it.

This is key: when Tögal is practiced correctly, even the densest thoughts do not obstruct — they **reflect the natural clarity of Rigpa**, awakened awareness. The practitioner dwells continuously in this mode during the **guiding instructions on the Base**, devoting five, ten, or more days to this illumination.

This is the **thirteenth session** dedicated to transforming discursive thoughts on the path, following the words of the masters.

✦ 6. Continuous Presentation to Awake Presence

The **A-khrid** text leads to direct experience of **awakened presence** — not as a concept of Buddha, but as living, nondual realization. It explains that hearing or contemplating the View is not enough: it must be practiced, integrated, and ultimately embodied.

The **fruit** is nothing other than the natural ability to benefit beings from within the fullness of clarity.

> "Not only is there nothing outside the mind; all things are miraculous displays of the mind itself."

✦ 7. The Three Essential Presentations

These three insights are central to Tögal in the A-khrid system:

- **Appearances are mind**: Everything we see, feel, and experience is a manifestation of the play of mind.
- **Mind is boundless**: It has no form, no center, no edges. It cannot be captured by concepts.

- **This boundlessness is the Three Bodies** (*Trikāya*):
    - **Dharmakāya**: emptiness
    - **Sambhogakāya**: clarity
    - **Nirmāṇakāya**: spontaneous compassionate activity
      These are not separate entities but **simultaneous dimensions** of awakened presence.

✧ Commentary: The Radiant Vision of Dzogchen Tögal ✧

The **Atri system of Dzogchen** offers guidance that moves beyond conceptual effort and introduces us to the luminous, direct contemplation of **reality as it is**.

This is the heart of Tögal: **not something we do**, but a **spontaneous revelation of our true being**. The key is not to fix or improve the mind, but to **see it as already perfect in essence**.

Practice becomes a **complete trust in the spontaneity of what is**, a surrender to the inner light that — effortlessly — liberates all that arises.

✸ The Rainbow Body (Jalü)

The culmination of these paths may be the **manifestation of the rainbow body**, where the physical body **dissolves into light upon death**, leaving no corpse behind—only hair and nails. This is not symbolic: it is a documented phenomenon among realized Dzogchen masters like:

- **Shardza Tashi Gyaltsen** (Bön tradition)
- **Küntsang Yeshe** and others in the Buddhist Nyingma school

These beings didn't transcend death through dogma—but through mastering **Trekchö's recognition** and **Tögal's vision**.

> The *Great Perfection* does not promise heaven—it **reveals that we have never been separate from it**.

por Tagzig,

(རྫོགས་ཆེན་ཐོད་རྒལ་
རྩ་བའི་དགོངས་བཞེད་ལྟར་)

འོད་གསལ་ཐོད་རྒལ་གྱི་ཞལ་གདམས།
རྣམ་སྣང་གྱི་སྒྱུ་འཕྲུལ་འགྱུར་བའི་ཞལ་བཤད།

མེ་བ་འབར་བའི་ནམ་ཆར་པ་འབྱུང་། །
རྡོ་བའི་མི་སྨྱོན་པའི་ནམ་ནོར་བུ་འཁྱོལ། །
མཐའ་ཡས་སྟོང་པའི་ཞལ་ངག་ཅན་གྱིས་གཏོང་བ། །
ས་ཡི་རི་ནི་ཆེན་གསེར་བར་གྱུར་པ་ན།
མི་གཡོགས་པའི་མིག་གིས་མཐོང་བའི་ཚུལ་དུ།

གཏི་མུག་གི་གསེར་ཁྲིད་གཅིག་གིས།
དུད་འགྲོའི་མཐའ་མ་མཚམས་ལམ་བརྒྱབ། །
འདུག་སྤྱོད་ཀྱི་འདུད་སྤུན་གཅིག་གིས།
ཡིད་འཐུས་གྲོགས་མེད་འགྲོ་བ་བསྐོར།

ཡིད་ལ་ཞལ་འཛུག་འདི།
གཟུགས་མེད་པའི་དྲི་མ་མེད་པ། །
མཚེར་མེད་གདོང་སྟོང་བའི་ཡིད་འཆིག་གིས།
མ་བྱང་བའི་ལྟ་བ་ལས་བརྟན་དུ་འཆད།

ཐོད་རྒལ་འོད་ལས་སྣང་བ་མ་རྫུན། །
འོད་གསལ་རང་རིག་གི་རིས་མེད་རྣམ་པ། །

རིགས་ཀྱི་མེ་ལོང་། འཁྱིལ་སྒྲོན། དཀྱིལ་འཁོར། །
སྤྱན་ནོར་གྱི་འོད་ཟེར་དབྱིངས་ན་འབྱུང་། །
འདི་དག་ལ་ལྟ་ཡང་མ་འདྲས། །
བདེན་པར་མཐོང་ན་རང་ཉིད་ཡིན།

དགེ་སློང་དགའ་རབ་རྡོ་རྗེས་ཞལ་ལ་ཟླ་བའི་ཞལ་བཤ
ད།

"ཐམས་ཅད་རང་གི་ངོ་བོ་ཡིན།
རང་རང་བསམ་གཞིར་གནས།"

རྡོ་རྗེ་དཔའ་བོ་ཀློང་ཆེན་པས་གཞས་འབུལ།

"རང་སྣང་འདི་འབྱུང་བ་མེད་པ་དང་ཆད་པ་མེད་པ་ཡིན། །
ནམ་མཁའི་རྒྱན་གྱི་རིག་པ་རང་འདུས་འདི་འདྲ།"

ནམ་ཡང་མ་མཐོང་ན།
ཉི་མ་ནི་མེ་མཐེ་བ་དང་འདྲ། །
ཟླ་བ་ནི་གནོད་པའི་ངོ་བོ་འདྲ། །
རླུང་ནི་མཐེ་ཕྲུག་མཐུན་མེད་འདྲ།

ནས་གཞི་འགྱུར་བ། སྐུ་ལྟུགས། རྨི་ལམ། །
སྤྲུལ་སྐུའི་གནས་སྐབས་སྟོབས་མེད་ནས་བཟུང་།
རང་བཞིན་ལས་མ་རིག་པར་འབྱུང་བ་ལྟ་བུ།

དེ་བཞིན་ཡང་ཡོན་ཏན་འོད་ལྟ་བུས་སྣང་བ་ན།
གང་རུང་གི་འགྲོ་བ་མར་འགྲོ་མེད། །
འཁོར་འདས་ཡི་འཁྱིལ་འཛིག་མེད་ཡི་རྟོགས།

རང་རྒྱུད་ལས་འབྱུང་བའི་རིག་པ་མངོན་པའི་རི་བོ་ནས།
ཤར་རྗེ་མཁན་ཆེན་བདེ་བ་འབྲེལ་ཞིང་བཀྱིས།
"ལམ་མེད་ཀྱང་འཕྲོ་བ་ཡོད་པ་ལྟ་བུ།"

དེ་འདྲས་ན་ཁ་ཕྱེ་ཞིང་དུས་ཀྱི་དོན་གཏོང་།
མིང་བཤད་པ་མེད་པར་བཞག།
གདོང་སྟོང་པའི་སྣང་བ་ནས་འཛུལ།
རང་དང་གཞན་མིན་པ་ནང་སྐྱེས།
རང་ངོ་མ་བསྐོར་བའི་འོད་འདི་གཙོ།
རང་དུ་བལྟས་པ་ནས་འཛིགས་པ་མེད།
མ་ཚར་པ་མེད།

Transmutation of Appearances

(A Song of Luminous Tögal)

Where fire burns, water springs forth,
And where the stone lies mute,
A jewel arises, singing of emptiness.
The earth becomes the gold of heaven
When the eye sees without veil.
A single spark of ignorance
Ignites the whole of hell;
A single breeze of desire
Summons the hungry realms.
O mind! dancing reflection,
Bottomless mirror, wave without sea—
You who chase hollow forms,
Awaken to the undying radiance.

In the light of Tögal,
Vision is not fabrication:
It is the pure form
Of consciousness set free.
Visions arise—
Circles, rays, mandalas,
Oceans of light upon the heart.
But take them not for gods or traps:
They are you, formless and unnamed.

All is your own face shining—
Recognize it, and rest

Appearances neither arise nor cease,
They are the natural ornament of space.
If this is unseen,
Even the sun becomes a blade,
The moon, a demon's face,
And the breeze, an invisible knife.
Thus the dwellings shift,
The bodies, the dreams,
Like actors on a thousand stages
You built without knowing.
Yet when Presence shines,
All is clear, all is light.
No birth, no death—
Only the sacred play of emptiness.
From the peak of spontaneous knowing,
Shardza laughs with compassion:

"There is no path—
And yet, you can fly."
So drop the map,
Abandon the name,
Enter naked into direct vision,
Where there is no self nor other,
Only the Recognized Light
Beholding itself,
Untiring,
Endless.

But these visions are not the goal.

Tempa Dukte Lama:
"The visions are not the goal; recognizing their source as the natural mind is the essence."

Longchenpa:
"The play of appearances is the spontaneous presence of the ground—inseparable from its purity."

The key is to realize the inseparability of emptiness and appearance—every vision, every color, every flicker of light is none other than the radiant play (*tsal*) of awareness.

Through Tögal, the practitioner moves beyond conceptual mind into the luminous presence of wisdom—*rigpa*—experiencing the unfolding of the "Four Visions" (Snang Ba Zhi), culminating in the exhaustion of phenomena into the dharmakāya.

A Unified Vision: The Great Perfection

Where Trekchö reveals the empty sky of mind, Tögal reveals its rainbow display. Where Trekchö is the stillness of the ocean, Tögal is the shimmer of waves and sunlight upon it. Both are expressions of the same nondual awareness.

Namkhai Norbu Rinpoche:
"Dzogchen is the path of self-liberation—recognize, relax, and remain."

Keith Dowman:
"There is nothing to do, nowhere to go—just this, now, as it is."

The teachings of the Great Perfection remind us that realization is not a fabrication but a recognition. Not a journey outward, but an unveiling inward. As **Vimalamitra** taught:
"Primordial purity is not fabricated; spontaneous presence is the display of wisdom."

Spontaneity and Effortlessness

Longchenpa emphasizes that **Tögal is not a visualization practice**. The visions are not imagined—they are the **self-display of awareness itself**. He writes:

> "Pure mind is like the empty sky… unstirring, uncontrived… > One in view free of limiting elaboration, > One in meditation free of limiting ideation, > One in conduct free of limiting endeavor, > And one in fruition free of limiting attainment… > Vast! Spacious! Released as it stands!"

This is the heart of Dzogchen: **nothing to fabricate, nothing to abandon**. The path is not about striving, but about **recognizing what is already perfect**.

Practical Summary Table

Met hod	Focus	Key Practice	Realization
Trekchö	Primordial Purity (*Ka-dag*)	Effortless recognition and resting	Mind's unchanging, open essence
Tögal	Spontaneous Presence (*Lhun-drub*)	Visionary display, sky/dark retreat	Unity of emptiness and appearance

Voices of the Masters

His Holiness the 33rd Menri Trizin:

"The unborn state is not an attainment—it is the ground of all."

Menri Lopon Rinpoche:

"True meditation is not doing, but seeing—seeing what has always been."

Nangzher Löpo:
"Let the mind fall into itself—there, you will find the unborn purity."

Latri Nyima Dakpa Rinpoche:
"Do not follow the breath, follow awareness; do not chase light, become light."

Closing Reflection

To walk the path of Dzogchen is not to become enlightened—it is to awaken to the fact that enlightenment is already the case. Trekchö reveals the *ground*—empty, vast, and pure. Tögal reveals the *display*—radiant, luminous, and wise.

In the stillness and the vision, in the sky and its light, the Great Perfection dances silently.

Let go.
Rest.
Recognize.
This is it.

The Four Visions of Tögal – The Unfolding of Awakening

While **Trekchö** reveals the empty nature of being, **Tögal** unfolds its innate luminosity. This path, also called the *direct crossing* (*thod rgal*), introduces us to a living experience of Awakening: not as theory, but as direct vision. Here, the mind isn't sought or cut; it's contemplated shining as light.

These visions aren't ordinary illusions. They are revelations of the spontaneous wisdom of **Rigpa**, the clear recognition of our true nature. They unfold progressively through what the masters call *the Four Visions* (*snang ba bzhi*), which arise naturally by integrating the stability of Trekchö with the openness of Tögal. This precise unfolding has been transmitted through a continuous lineage, from **Garab Dorje** to contemporary masters like **Tenzin Wangyal Rinpoche**, ensuring its authenticity and profound efficacy.

○ First Vision: The Emergence of Direct Appearance (*snang ba tong tsam*)

Description: Lights, flashes, colored spheres, and subtle forms like wheels, vajra crosses, or rainbow mandalas appear. These aren't external objects but manifestations of clarity itself. They are experienced by gazing at the sky, a luminous surface, or within a dark retreat.

Essence: Appearing and seeing unify. The senses don't seek externally; they invert towards the source of light. There's no judgment or interpretation—only radiant presence. This is the initial unveiling of **Lhun-drub**, the spontaneous display, from the **Ka-dag** ground.

Padmasambhava: *"Seeing light without searching, recognizing without fabricating: this is the wisdom that arises from emptiness."*

Practice:

- **Sky-gazing** (*namkha artal*): a relaxed gaze into the open sky.
- Recognize that colors and visions arise from **Rigpa**, not from the eye. This mirrors the instruction of **Vimalamitra**, who emphasized recognizing the illusory nature of all appearances.

□ Second Vision: The Increase of Experience (*nyam gyur bar snang*)

Description: The visions become more vivid and organized: complete mandalas, light deities, geometric forms that multiply, rotate, and merge. They can expand and fill the entire visual field.

Essence: The energy of the luminous mind is recognized as non-dual with emptiness. Forms don't distract; they reveal. Perception purifies, and it's understood that all appearance is a play of awakened consciousness. This stage deepens the experience of **Rang-byung Yeshe**, the self-arising wisdom.

Longchenpa: *"Nothing appears outside of wisdom. The vision increases, not by effort, but by openness."*

Practice:

- Deepen non-elaboration.
- Don't pursue visions, don't resist them. Let them unfold naturally, like **flowers blooming from emptiness**. This effortless unfolding is a key instruction from masters like **Jigme Lingpa**.

□ Third Vision: The Fullness of Realization (*mthar phyin pa'i snang ba*)

Description: Mandalas stabilize. There's a direct understanding: everything that appears is wisdom. Complete deities and radiant light mandalas emerge, along with a state of unconditioned bliss. It's as if the entire universe vibrates with sacred meaning.

Essence: The practitioner no longer separates subject and object. All appearance is an expression of self-luminous wisdom. The **unity of emptiness and form** is realized as inseparable. The self dissolves into the free play of **Rigpa**. This stage marks a profound integration of the **Ground** (*gzhi*) as described by masters like **Menri Lopon Rinpoche** and **Latri Nyima Dakpa Rinpoche**.

Mipham Rinpoche: *"What was formerly seen as external is now recognized as the unfolding of the luminous self."*

Practice:

- Integrate vision and meditation.
- Don't seek to maintain the vision: even its disappearance is perfect. This non-clinging is crucial, as taught by **Jamyang Khyentse Wangpo**, ensuring that the experience leads to liberation, not attachment.

● Fourth Vision: The Natural Exhaustion of All Phenomena (*rang zhi thim pa'i snang ba*)

Description: The visions spontaneously dissolve. There is no more need for form, light, or experience. Everything exhausts itself into non-appearance, not as a dry void, but as omnipresent wisdom without the need for form. Here, the **dharmakāya** is fully realized.

Essence: The cycle of vision culminates in the total liberation of dualistic perception. What remains is not nothingness, but the non-conceptual fullness of Awakening. The body dissolves into light or is recognized as unreal from its origin. This ultimate **self-liberation (*rang grol*)** is the pinnacle of the path.

Garab Dorje: *"When nothing remains to be seen, there is nothing to lose. The end is the beginning without beginning."* This perfectly encapsulates the return to primordial purity (**Ka-dag**).

Practice:

- No technique is necessary.
- Simply rest in the spontaneity of wisdom, like **a river naturally merging into the ocean**. This complete

letting go is the final instruction, reflecting the teachings of **Jnanasutra** and **Shri Singha**.

Mystical Synthesis: Awakening as Vision

Vision	Tibetan Name	Spiritual Synthesis
1. Appearance	*snang ba tong tsam*	Light arises from emptiness as pure play
2. Increase	*nyam gyur bar snang*	Visions expand, but are not separate from Being
3. Fullness	*mthar phyin pa'i snang ba*	Everything is recognized as spontaneous wisdom
4. Exhaustion	*rang zhi thim pa'i snang ba*	Everything dissolves into the unborn space of reality

The Manifestation of the Rainbow Body

When a practitioner fully realizes **Tögal**, they may attain **Jalu**, the **Rainbow Body**. In this state, the **physical body dissolves into light**, leaving behind only **hair and nails**.

Historical Accounts

- **Shardza Tashi Gyaltsen**, a **Bön master**, consciously attained the **Body of Light**. He taught: *"That which is empty and luminous does not die; it simply releases itself from its temporary form."*
- **Padmasambhava**, **Longchenpa**, and **Garab Dorje** are said to have **transcended form**, revealing the **inseparability of emptiness and luminosity**.

Philosophical Significance

- **Union of Emptiness and Light**: Jalu is the **final manifestation** of reality—**empty yet radiant**.
- **Beyond Birth and Death**: The body is **an illusion**, and realization **transcends form**.
- **Effortless Realization**: Jalu is **not achieved through effort** but through **resting in the natural state**.

The Purpose of Tögal

✔ **Integral Transformation**: Tögal **transforms body, energy, and perception** beyond intellect.

✔ **Conscious Death**: It prepares the practitioner to **die in full awareness**, free from conditioned rebirth.

✓ **Universal Service**: Realizing **Totality**, one becomes a **living channel of wisdom and compassion**.

Conclusion: Beyond Light, Only Reality

The **Dzogchen path** has **no beginning or end**. Visions **cease**, the **body dissolves**, but what remains is **not a thing**—it is **Reality itself recognizing itself through you**.

"There is nothing to attain, because what you are cannot be lost." — **Padmasambhava** *"There is no enlightenment apart from this moment as it is."* — **Keith Dowman**

This refined version integrates **Longchenpa's wisdom**, Tögal's **visionary path**, and the **Rainbow Body phenomenon**, offering a **comprehensive contemplative guide**. Let me know if you'd like further refinements or additions.

Practical Application in Dzogchen Practice

The path of Dzogchen is often divided into two main approaches, which complement each other:

Tögal (*thod rgal*): This practice, as described by the Four Visions, involves **"direct crossing"** or engaging with the **Spontaneous Presence (Lhun-drub)**. It's about allowing the innate luminosity and spontaneous display of **Rigpa** to manifest directly through one's senses, particularly vision. It's the dynamic aspect where the **unity of Ka-dag (emptiness) and Lhun-drub (clarity)** is realized experientially. While Trekchö establishes the sky's openness, Tögal lets us witness the **rainbows and sunbeams** that spontaneously arise within that openness, without staining it. Masters like **Chökyi Nyima Rinpoche** and **Khandro Rinpoche** guide practitioners through these luminous experiences as a natural outcome of stable Trekchö practice.

Tögal is not a psychedelic journey, nor a visual theater. It is the recognition of wisdom as light, and of light as emptiness. The visions are **mirrors of Rigpa**; they aren't pursued, but are allowed to liberate themselves naturally. This understanding is key to the Dzogchen lineage, shared across both Nyingma and Bön traditions, from **Nangzher Löpo** to **His Holiness the Yongzin Tenzin Namdak who lived in bliss up to a 100 years.**

The seer, the seen, and the act of seeing...

...merge like **rainbows in the cloudless sky**, leaving no trace, just boundless purity. As **Keith Dowman** eloquently reminds us, the essence lies in this seamless integration and effortless being.

The Four Gazes and Three Postures in Tögal: Unveiling Innate Luminosity

The **Tögal** (*thod rgal*) practice in Dzogchen, meaning "direct crossing," is a profound method for directly experiencing the **innate luminosity of Rigpa**. Unlike **Trekchö**, which emphasizes recognizing the emptiness of being, Tögal actively engages with **Spontaneous Presence (Lhun-drub)** to realize the indivisible unity of **primordial purity (Ka-dag)** and this inherent radiance. This path involves specific gazes and postures, not as strenuous techniques, but as subtle means to facilitate the natural arising of visionary experiences.

These instructions are rooted in the wisdom passed down by highly authoritative masters, from **Longchenpa** and **Padmasambhava, or Taphiritza** to contemporary teachers such as, **Tenzin Wangyal Rinpoche**, **Yongzin Tenzin Namdak Rinpoche**.

The Four Gazes: Gateways to Vision

The "four gazes" (sometimes referred to as the "four lamps" or "four seals") are progressive ways of directing the eyes and awareness to facilitate the arising of inner visions. They are designed to subtlely shift perception, allowing the innate light of Rigpa to manifest.

1. **Gazing into Infinite Space (Sky Gazing):**

    - **Description:** The practitioner gazes with **relaxed, unfocused eyes** into the open sky during the day or at a luminous, vast surface. The aim is to allow awareness to **merge with space itself**, becoming boundless and unconfined.
    - **Purpose:** This gaze primarily facilitates the emergence of the foundational "empty luminosity," allowing the mind's true nature to be seen as vast and unobstructed, like the **unclouded sky**. It purifies conceptual elaborations.

2. **Gazing at a Luminous Object:**

    - **Description:** The gaze is directed at a source of light, such as the sun (with extreme care and guidance, typically at dawn or dusk), the moon, or a lamp. This is usually done at a specific distance, often about one cubit (forearm length) from the object, allowing the light to enter directly.
    - **Purpose:** This gaze helps to **stimulate the arising of vibrant colored lights, spheres**

(thigles), and subtle forms within the visual field. It specifically engages with the luminous aspect of Rigpa, allowing its inner radiance to become manifest.

3. **Gazing into Darkness:**

    - **Description:** Performed in a completely dark retreat setting or in total darkness at night, the practitioner gazes into the pervasive absence of external light.
    - **Purpose:** This method encourages the **arising of inner light visions** spontaneously from within, revealing that the luminosity of Rigpa is inherent and doesn't depend on external light sources. It's a powerful way to access the mind's self-illuminating nature.

4. **Gazing at the Tip of the Nose or Between the Eyebrows:**

    - **Description:** The gaze is gently directed downwards towards the tip of the nose or slightly upwards towards the point between the eyebrows (the third eye area). This is a subtle, almost internal focus.
    - **Purpose:** This specific direction of gaze helps to **stabilize inner vision and awareness**, consolidating the experiences from the other gazes. It can refine the clarity and presence of internal manifestations.

Crucial Guidelines for All Gazes:

- **Relaxation is Paramount:** The gaze should always be **relaxed, never forced or tense**. Any strain will hinder the arising of natural visions.
- **Partial Openness:** The eyes are typically kept **partially open**, not fully closed (which can lead to dullness) nor wide open (which can create tension). This allows for a subtle interaction with light while maintaining inner focus.
- **Gentle Breath:** The breath should be **gentle and natural**, often through the mouth with lips slightly parted. This helps relax the facial muscles and allows the subtle energies (lung/prana) to flow freely.

The Three Postures: Aligning Body and Energy

Complementing the gazes, there are three classic postures (sometimes referred to as the "rishi's postures" or "body gates") used in Tögal practice. Each posture subtly influences the flow of internal energy and facilitates different aspects of visionary experience. They are designed to naturally open the subtle channels and allow **Rigpa's luminosity** to manifest without obstruction.

1. **Dharmakaya Posture:**
   - **Description:** Sitting cross-legged, often in full lotus with the soles of the feet pointing upwards. The back is straight but relaxed, and the hands typically rest in the lap, or sometimes support the cheeks with the palms.
   - **Purpose:** This posture is traditionally said to **balance bliss and emptiness**, and to naturally block "impure apertures," leading to a profound sense of inner equilibrium conducive to the arising of primordial wisdom. It helps to stabilize the very ground of being.
2. **Sambhogakaya Posture:**
   - **Description:** Sitting with one knee raised (often the right knee) and the opposite arm resting on it, while the other hand rests on the ground or the knee.
   - **Purpose:** This posture is generally more **relaxed and open**, specifically supporting the **arising of visionary experiences** by facilitating the

outward flow of subtle energy and light. It helps to manifest the spontaneous radiance of Rigpa.

3. **Nirmanakaya (Rishi's) Posture:**

    - **Description:** This refers to various crouching or semi-crouching postures. Examples include sitting with elbows and knees on the ground, or with one leg folded and the other extended. These can be alternated for comfort and to adjust the energetic flow.
    - **Purpose:** This posture type can be specifically alternated to **facilitate different visionary experiences** and to work with various energy blockages, allowing for deeper engagement with the Tögal process. It's often used for its dynamic properties in revealing light.

Universal Posture Guidelines:

- **Relaxed Spine:** The spine should always remain **relaxed yet naturally straight**, allowing the central channel to be unobstructed.
- **No Tension:** The body should **not be tense**; comfort and profound relaxation are absolutely essential for the visions to arise naturally and for awareness to remain spacious.
- **Hand Positions:** Hands may rest on the knees, in the lap, or support the cheeks, depending on the specific posture and the guidance of one's teacher.

Integration and Practice: Effortless Unfolding

It's important to understand that you do not need to use all postures or gazes in every session. A qualified Dzogchen teacher will provide precise guidance on which gazes and postures are appropriate for an individual practitioner's stage and needs. Choose what naturally supports the arising of clear light and what feels comfortable, as **forcing will only create obstacles**.

The key to all Tögal practice is to **rest in a relaxed, open state**, allowing visions to arise and dissolve naturally, **without grasping or fabrication**. The practice is always rooted in the recognition of **Rigpa**, the natural state, as the fundamental basis and source for all visionary experience. It's like **waiting for the dawn**, knowing the sun will rise without any effort on your part; you just need to be open to its light.

References to the Great Masters

The principles of the Four Gazes and Three Postures are deeply embedded in the Dzogchen tradition. They are meticulously detailed in the classic texts and oral instructions stemming from early Indian Masters like **Garab Dorje**, **Manjushrimitra**, **Shri Singha**, **Jnanasutra**, and **Vimalamitra**. These teachings were then powerfully transmitted to Tibet by **Padmasambhava**, **Vairotsana**, and **Yeshe Tsogyal**.

Tögal is not about effort or constructing visions, but about **relaxing deeply, opening awareness, and letting the innate luminosity of mind display itself**. It's the **spontaneous manifestation of the Real**, seen through the purification of the senses.

Summary Table

Gaze Type	Description	Purpose
Sky Gazing	Eyes relaxed, gaze into open sky or luminous surface	Merge awareness with infinite space; purify concepts
Luminous Object Gazing	Gaze at sun/moon/lamp (with care)	Facilitate arising of colored lights/forms; engage luminosity
Darkness Gazing	Gaze into darkness (night or dark retreat)	Allow inner light visions to arise spontaneously
Nose/Forehead Gazing	Gaze downward (nose tip) or between eyebrows	Stabilize inner vision and awareness; refine manifestations

Posture Type	Description	Purpose
Dharmakaya Posture	Cross-legged, hands in lap or on cheeks	Balance bliss/emptiness; block impure apertures; stabilize ground
Sambhogakaya Posture	One knee raised, opposite arm resting on it	Relaxed, open; supports arising of visionary experiences
Nirmanakaya (Rishi's) Posture	Crouching or semi-crouching; varied leg/arm positions	Facilitates different visionary experiences; works with energy flow

In essence: The four gazes and three postures of Tögal are practical gateways for the spontaneous display of awareness. Their purpose is not to create visions, but to **reveal the natural radiance of Rigpa**, the true nature of mind, by resting in effortless presence. They provide a precise framework for the **direct recognition of your innate wisdom and luminosity**.

Jalu: The Manifestation of the Rainbow Body

When a practitioner fully realizes the **Four Visions of Tögal**, they may attain **Jalu**, the **Rainbow Body**. In this state, the **physical body dissolves completely into light** at the moment of death—or even before—leaving behind only hair and nails.

One of the most well-documented cases of this phenomenon is **Shardza Tashi Gyaltsen**, a great **Bön master of the 20th century**, who consciously attained the **Body of Light**. He taught:

"That which is empty and luminous does not die; it simply releases itself from its temporary form."

Jalu: Beyond Attainment, the Natural Unfolding of Realization

The Rainbow Body and the Three Kayas

When Tögal is practiced to completion, the practitioner may realize the **three kayas**:

- **Dharmakaya** – the empty, formless essence
- **Sambhogakaya** – the luminous visionary expression
- **Nirmanakaya** – the compassionate activity in the world

This realization may culminate in the **rainbow body (jalü)**, where the physical body dissolves into light at death. Longchenpa affirms that this is not a myth, but the **natural fruition of resting in rigpa and allowing its radiance to unfold**.

Jalu is **not a goal to be pursued**, but rather the **natural result** of the **complete integration of wisdom and compassion** within the **body and mind**. It signifies that **essence, presence, and energy** have unified beyond the limitations of ego.

In the **Dzogchen tradition**, the dissolution into light is seen as the **ultimate expression of realization**, where the practitioner transcends the physical realm, revealing the **inseparability of emptiness and luminosity**.

Longchenpa on Tögal: The Light Revealed Within

In his masterwork *The Precious Treasury of the Basic Space of Phenomena* (*Chöying Dzö*), Longchenpa offers not only philosophical depth but intimate instruction on **how the radiance of awareness unfolds** when left unaltered. Here's a rendering that stays close to the tone of his transmission:

> "Like stars appearing in a clear night sky, > The display of awareness arises naturally— > Without effort, without fabrication, > Pure appearance, self-luminous and unconfined."

These visions are not imagined projections. They are **innate radiances**—manifestations of the very fabric of awareness (*rigpa*). Tögal doesn't introduce something new—it simply **unveils what was always present**.

What makes Dzogchen, and Tögal in particular, so radical is Longchenpa's **refusal to separate the ordinary from the sacred**. The same appearances that delude, when seen from rigpa, **liberate themselves**.

He writes:

> *"This present moment— > whatever appears within it— > is the effortless mandala of the awakened state."*

In Tögal, even form, sound, and thought are **pure expressions of the enlightened mind**. Nothing needs to be changed. The veil drops not because we clear it away—but because it was never real to begin with.

If you'd like, I can lead you through a poetic sequence—an experiential tour—of the **Four Visions** as meditated and described by Longchenpa. Or I can draw parallels with Jigme Lingpa's transmission in the Longchen Nyingthig. We can even map this into a retreat-style journey.

🌀 The Play of the Four Visions in Light of Longchenpa's Writings

1. **Apparent Reality Emerges Naturally** Longchenpa writes that the first glimpses are like "bubbles shimmering on water," delicate and transient. These rainbow thigles and light formations **emerge effortlessly** when resting in open presence—especially in practices like sky-gazing.
2. **The Display Intensifies** With continuity of practice, the visions deepen. "Mandalas unfold, not constructed but self-born." According to Longchenpa, these are "the ornaments of empty clarity," expressions of awareness moving within itself.
3. **The Mandala Becomes Vast** This stage reveals an "infinite cathedral of presence," where pure forms—deities, dakinis, sacred geometry—**reside within the expanse of timeless mind**.
4. **The Display Dissolves into Reality** Eventually, all appearances dissolve back into openness. "Not through

cessation, but through self-liberation," as Longchenpa would say. This is the **true seeing of the nature of mind**, free of perceiver and perceived.

🌈 From Vision to Fruition: The Rainbow Body

For Longchenpa, the full path culminates in the *Great Completion*—where the union of Trekchö and Tögal **transmutes the body into light**. It's said that such a master can, at the time of death, dissolve all physical form into space, leaving behind only hair and nails. This is **not metaphor**, but lived reality in the lives of yogis like **Padmasambhava**, **Vimalamitra**, and later, **Shardza Rinpoche**.

གནས་གྱི་དོན་དུ་རྣམ་དག་གི་སྣང་བ། །

སྣང་བ་དང་སྒྲ་དང་རྣམ་རྟོག་གསལ་གྱི་རྫས། ། གཟ

鏡་གང་གི་འདྲས་བར་མཚུངས་ཞིག་ཡིན། །

དེའི་རང་བཞིན་མ་རྟོགས་ན་འཁྱོལ་ཞིང་བདག་བརྒྱབ

། །

རིག་པ་མ་ཤེས་པའི་དགའ་སྟོན་ནས། །སྣང་བ་གང་ཅང་གིས་འཁོར་བའི་ཁམས་དྲུགས། །
ཁྲིས་པ་དེ་བར་དུ་མི་འཛིགས་གཞིས། །སེམས་པ་ནས་འཆི་མེད་བར་དུ་འཁྱོལ་ལྡོག་མི་བྱ། །

ཐོད་རྒྱལ་ནང་ནས་གྲིད་པའི་ནམ་མཁའ། །རང་གི་འོད་ཟེར་རང་བཞིན་དང་ནས་གྲོལ། །
དགོངས་པ་མི་འགྱུར་གི་བལྟ་བས་རིག་པ་ལ་ཞུགས། །གཟུང་འཛིན་མེད་པ་འདུས་མ་བྱས་པར་འགྲོ་བ།

།འཁྲུལ་པ་རང་གི་རྟོགས་པར་འདུག་གསུངས། ། མེ་ལས་བྱུས་པའི་སྣང་བ་བཞིན་དུ་སྣང་ཞིང་། །
དག་མེད་པ་ཡི་སྣང་བ་མ་མཚུངས་ཡིན་ཞིང་། ། ཁྱད་པར་མེད་པའི་རིག་པ་འདི་ན་བཞུགས། །

The Light Within Appears

When mind forgets its sky-like ground, a single shadow births a storm. Form becomes fear, sound becomes sorrow, thought—confusion that multiplies.

Yet all that flickers in the dark was only ever luminous, a mirror playing at shape and color— empty and clear.

The master said: *"Don't fix it. Don't chase it. Just see."*

In Tögal's gaze, light rises from within: circles of fire, rainbows without rain, visions that sing without sound.

Not fantasy. Not dream. But the wisdom that dances when rigpa rests.

The stones turn gold. The fire cools into water. The walls of the world grow translucent— not because matter is changed, but because *perception is unbound.*

This is not escape. Not ascent.

It is revelation.

The yogi sits, body still as mountain, eye open to the inner sky.

What comes—he does not grasp. What leaves—she does not mourn.

All is light. All is mind. All is the sacred play of knowing.

And when even this display dissolves, what remains is so simple: a Presence that needs no proof to be real.

Poem by Tagzig

I. Appearances as the Magic of Space

When Presence is not recognized, a single image, sound, or thought can plunge the mind into confusion. A form can become a threat; an emotion, a storm. At that point, appearances become gateways to the six realms of samsara:

- **Anger** generates hellish visions.
- **Desire** causes rebirth in the realm of hungry ghosts.
- **Ignorance** gives rise to the animal realm.
- **Jealousy and envy** pull one into the asura (demigod) worlds.
- **Pride** fuels rebirth among the gods.
- **Greed** binds one to the human realm.

As explained by **Nangzher Löpo** in his tantric treatises, and realized by great sages of the Bön tradition like **Yongdzin Tenzin Namdak Rinpoche**, even in states like sleep or intoxication, appearances reflect karma and mental imprints in action.

The Light of Pure Vision

In the practice of Tögal, the goal is not to eliminate appearances, but to recognize them as expressions of the luminosity inherent in awareness. This recognition begins with spontaneous visions of light: points, rays, colored circles, and radiant shapes that arise during contemplative gazing.

A-khrid: Inner Alchemy – Gold, Water, Light

In the state of realization, **stones turn to turquoise, earth into gold, fire into water**—not because their elements change, but because **perception is purified at its root**. The awakened mind sees everything as an expression of the same luminous source.

This is what ancient alchemists called transmutation—and what **Shardza Tashi Gyaltsen** described as the manifestation of primordial vision.

The ordinary mind chases appearances, generating endless karma. But the yogi who rests in rigpa, as **Jigme Lingpa** taught, ceases the chase and allows everything to **liberate at its origin**. As **Tenzin Wangyal Rinpoche** states, there is no separation between **appearance and emptiness**, between **form and light**.

The Luminous Play of the Mind

Even when the body sleeps, space fills with dancing forms. In Tögal practice, these visions are recognized as wisdom itself. The advanced yogi neither clings to them nor rejects them. They understand that all appearances—be they monsters or deities, celestial landscapes or flaming hells—are like dreams.

As **Jamgon Kongtrul Lodrö Thaye** taught: > "The sage views samsara and nirvana as illusions of the same dream."

Thus, step by step, **the mind settles, the vision clarifies**, and **the heart rests in the unshakable certainty of the natural state**: luminous, empty, present.

This is the gift of Tögal—not to transcend the world, but to **transmute it from the root**, recognizing that it has never been other than yourself, **free from the beginning**.

Dzogchen Contemplative Guide: The Path of Effortless Recognition

I. Guruyoga: The Foundation of Practice

Begin with **Guruyoga**, the **Yoga of Union**, a simple yet profound practice. You may firmly say **Hung**, recite **Divine Names**, or any **prayer that inspires you**. This invocation aligns your mind with the **natural state**, preparing you for deeper contemplation.

Following this, engage in **purifying breaths**, such as **Pranayama** or the **Nine Purifications**, to clear energetic blockages and harmonize your inner flow.

GuruYoga

🙏 **Prayer of Aspiration**

"Master, God, or Buddha, —bless me so May I realize myself as Buddha, Awakened from illusion, Abiding in the clear light of my true nature— For the benefit of all beings." ༔

□□ **Prāṇāyāma: Descending Breath into Silence**

Take **9 purifying breaths** or **9 deep long, slow and deep breaths**. With each breath, allow thoughts to settle. With each exhale, drop deeper—into stillness, into presence, into the vastness that holds all things. Now begin.

Union with the Master – Light of the Three Syllables

Sit quietly, **spine straight**. Your **body becomes a mountain.** Your **breath is the wind** whispering across its slopes. Your **heart opens like the sky**.

Above you, the **heavens part**. From the great expanse of timeless space, a **radiant being** appears— **Jesus**, embodiment of boundless love, or **Kuntuzangpo**, Buddha of innate purity—the essence of all awakened masters: past, present, and yet to come. He or She rests in meditation, surrounded in **rainbow light**, serene and immeasurable. From their heart, a stream of light descends—directly to you.

You whisper the sacred syllables:

Say ཨ **A three times.**

A single syllable resounds from the sky, — **Light touches the crown** of your head, blessing your body and chakras. It flows through your **central channel**, filling your **side channels** and all the **subtle currents** of your light-body. A whisper of infinity. **Birthless. Pure. Still.**

Note: You may say also also receive fire, wind and water blessing.

Say ཨ **A x 3 times.**

Another ray of light touches your **forehead**. It dissolves into your **mind-stream**, revealing **vast openness** and the silence beyond thought. Here: nothing to fix. Nothing to fear. Just *clarity without center.*

Say ཨོཾ **OM x 3 times.**

The light flows into your **throat**, seat of **speech**, **truth**, and **vibration**. A hum awakens—OM— and your voice aligns with **divine clarity**. No need to speak—your silence is prayer.

Say ཧཱུྃ **HUNG x 3 times.**

The light drops into your **heart center**, **gateway of compassion** and wisdom. There, it becomes a **sphere of radiant light**, pulsing gently with timeless knowing. Your being floods with **bliss**— not pleasure, but union.
Your master smiles, then transforms **into five-colored light**, a luminous sphere descending your **central channel** and resting within your heart **dissolving**. There is no separation. Your enlightened nature is revealed as **your own true face**.
Everything dissolves. Only **light and space remain**.
The master above and your own presence become one field: **sky in sky. light in light. being in being.**
Recognition dawns: **Boundless space. Luminous awareness. Unceasing joy.**
༔ Nothing to hold. ༔ Nothing to reject. ༔ Just this—*luminosity knowing itself.*
In Bon tradidition it is practiced, OM the thought but in other Tibetan traditions is practiced A and on the forehead OM.

II. Rainbow Breathing: Cultivating Inner Radiance

This exercise energizes the **central channel** and connects you with the **pure luminosity of Rigpa**. It is a simple yet powerful method to awaken your **inner light**.

The Practice

1. **Preparation**
    - Sit comfortably with a **naturally upright spine**.
    - If trained in **Shiné (Shamatha)**, keep your gaze **soft and open**. If not, gently lower your gaze. If drowsy, lift your eyes slightly.
    - If practicing **sky-gazing**, keep your eyes **fully open**.
2. **Inhaling the Rainbow**
    - Visualize your **two energy channels (nadis)** running parallel to your spine.
    - As you inhale deeply, imagine a **stream of radiant rainbow light** entering through the **nostrils**, flowing into these channels.
    - This is not mere air—it is **lung (vital energy)**, infused with the **vibrant spectrum of existence**.
3. **Fusion and Ascent**
    - The rainbow light **merges** into a **brilliant sphere** at the **base of your central channel** (below the navel or at the root chakra).
    - With each breath, **gently guide** this sphere **upward** through the **central channel**, clearing obstructions.
4. **Radiance at the Crown**

    - As the sphere ascends, it **illuminates each energy center (chakra)**.
    - Pause briefly at the **heart, throat, and third eye**, feeling their activation.
    - Finally, guide the **sphere to the crown**, where it **radiates outward**.
5. **Exhaling and Expanding**
    - As you exhale, visualize the **sphere dissolving** into the **vast, boundless space**.
    - Feel it **merging with universal luminosity**, releasing all tension and obscurations.

Key Points for Deepening the Experience

- **Purity of Color**: Each hue is **vibrant and flawless**, reflecting the **unconditioned nature** of your energy.
- **Effortless Ascent**: Let the energy **rise naturally**, like a **feather floating in still air**.
- **Sustained Visualization**: Keep the **image vivid** throughout the practice.
- **Feeling the Flow**: Beyond seeing, **sense the warmth, clarity, and vibrancy** of the light.
- **Connection with Rigpa**: Recognize that this **rainbow light** is an **expression of Rigpa**, not something created but **revealed**.

This practice purifies and **balances your energy system**, fostering **inner peace, clarity, and vitality**. It is a **direct experience** of the **spontaneous luminosity** always present within you.

III. Tögal: The Visionary Path of Light

Tögal is the **direct crossing** into **spontaneous presence (Lhun-drub)**. It unfolds through **Four Visions**, revealing the **inseparability of emptiness and light.**

1. Unification of the Three Spaces

- External **(the sky), the heart**, and **your gaze** merge into one.
- Feel the **vast openness**, free from fear.
- Let your **gaze rest**, like a **bird floating in clear wind.**
- Use **Hung, Phet, or A** to return to the **natural state.**

2. Let Light Reveal Itself

- Do not **seek meaning**—allow **light to manifest.**
- Forms will **arise and dissolve**, like **waves in an endless ocean.**

3. Neither Chase Nor Reject Visions

- They are **playful expressions of luminous emptiness.**
- Signs that **space itself has begun to sing.**

4. If a Deity Appears, Greet Without Attachment

- If **light emerges**, do not **possess it.**
- Recognize **everything as your own awakened face.**

5. In the End, Your Body Becomes Light

- There is **nowhere to go.**
- You **become the space itself, formless and boundless.**

Appearances: Manifestations of Pure Mind in the Light of Tögal

True alchemy does not consist in transmuting metals, but in recognizing the luminous essence of all appearances. When mind and phenomena are revealed as a single essence — the naked nature of reality — then earth becomes gold, stones become turquoise, fire becomes water, and poison becomes medicine. Everything is effortlessly transformed into a pure expression of awakened awareness.

In the cycle of Tögal — the direct crossing into reality as it is — a profound truth is revealed: appearances and mind share one luminous essence, and that essence is none other than **Rigpa**, Pure Presence, empty and awake. This is not an idea or belief, but a direct experience unveiled when dualistic grasping ceases.

This is the hidden power of direct vision (Tögal), where inner light manifests as self-arising visions that do not depend on external conditions. In Longchenpa's words: "Appearances are the spontaneous ornamentation of radiant emptiness." Here, mind and phenomenon are not separate: they are light-plays in the mirror of Rigpa.

Yet when this realization has not occurred, even a single appearance can disturb the ignorant mind and cast it into the abyss of suffering. If a mind blinded by karma falls into the hell dimension, all appearances turn into fire, knives, screams, and thorns. If it enters the realm of hungry spirits, every form is an unreachable feast, every sound an empty promise. Thus arise the six realms of samsara: projections of accumulated karmic patterns, from which unenlightened beings cannot free themselves.

Even now, in human life, this principle is manifest. When conceptual consciousness is distorted — in dreams, possession, fever, intoxication, or under the influence of substances or emotions — appearances twist. Double moons are seen, a rope is mistaken for a snake, voices are heard that do not exist. Unreality is taken for reality, and thus one falls deeper into illusion.

Shardza Tashi Gyaltsen (1859–1933 or 1935) was one of the greatest Dzogchen masters within the Tibetan Bön tradition. He is widely recognized for having attained the rainbow body, a spiritual phenomenon where the physical body dissolves into light at death, leaving only hair and nails.

He taught that in Tögal, the visions of rainbows, dancing lights, and floating mandalas are not illusions but the natural expression of the clear mind when afflictive interferences cease. Yet without recognition, even sacred visions may become traps if interpreted through the ego.

(*The Self-Dawning of the Three Bodies* (sku gsum rang shar): A profound Dzogchen text on the realization of the three kayas.) (*Commentary on Trul Khor*: a detailed explanation of yogic energy practices in the Bön tradition.)

Born in Kham, eastern Tibet, Shardza was a scholar, meditator, and prolific author whose teachings transcended his own tradition: he attracted disciples from both Bön and Tibetan Buddhist schools. Ordained a monk at 30, he wrote major philosophical and practical works, including commentaries on *Trul Khor*, a form of Tibetan yogic energy practice.

Shardza was also known for his strict ethical conduct: he was vegetarian and avoided harming any living being. His integrative approach and deep spiritual realization made him a central figure in modern Bön.

The Magical Display of the Clear Mind

All we see is, in truth, the magical display of the mind. By clinging to this play without recognizing its empty, luminous nature, we wander through existences, endlessly circling in samsara. Yet not a single one of these appearances possesses intrinsic existence: they are reflections, like dreams of a sleeping mind.

Where is the creator of these visions, these worlds, these karmic webs? Not outside. Here: in your own **Presence**. In your **Rigpa**, the awakened awareness beyond birth and death.

Due to these appearances, mind strays, agitates, and chases after the insubstantial, losing its natural rest. So it has happened in countless past lives: unknowingly falling again and again under the sway of illusions, projections, attachments, and rejections born of ignorance.

For all beings immersed in the deep sleep of non-recognition, all appearances — no matter how vivid, painful, or beautiful — are like mirages in the desert, reflections in water, dancing figures in a dream no one dreams.

We must see the nature of mind as it is, unfabricated.

Yongdzin Lopön Tenzin Namdak Rinpoche says: "It is not enough to understand that everything is illusion. One must see, in direct experience, how illusion reveals itself as wisdom."

And in Tögal practice, this wisdom appears as pure visions arising from the central channel, spontaneous reflections of the light of wisdom. It is not a visual game, but a gradual process of the liberation of appearances, until all merges into great clarity.

According to the *Lung Drug*: "These phenomena, without ground or origin, Appear according to how they are imagined."

Commentary: Appearances as Space Magic

When Presence has not been recognized, a single image, sound, sensation, or thought can confuse the mind and entangle it in samsaric nets. A neutral appearance may become a threat, an emotion a prison. At that point, appearances become gateways into the six realms of cyclic becoming:

- Anger crystallizes torment and aggression: the hell realm.
- Insatiable desire shapes the hungry ghost realm.
- Deep ignorance manifests the animal realm: closed and automatic.
- Jealousy and rivalry drag into the asura realm: constant conflict.
- Pride nourishes the god realm: intoxicated by ephemeral power.
- Greed and attachment construct the human realm: a mix of suffering and liberation potential.

Thus taught **Nangzher Löpo**, early Bön master, and clearly explained by **Yongdzin Lopön Tenzin Namdak Rinpoche**, who showed that even in dreams, intoxication, or hallucination, appearances are but reflections of karma and mental imprints.

Pure Vision on the Tögal Path

In Tögal, appearances are not rejected but recognized as manifestations of the pure light of consciousness. During practice, when gazing into the sky with half-open eyes, dots of light, rays, circles, and spontaneous mandalas arise. These are not imagined visions, but direct revelations of Rigpa's luminous potential. Described in the oral instruction cycle by **Padmasambhava** and transmitted by **Vairotsana** and **Yeshe Tsogyal**.

Longchen Rabjam wrote that these visions are like reflections in a mirror: not self-existing, but not mere illusions either. They are the play of consciousness in its pure state, like a rainbow effortlessly appearing in the open sky.

Tögal and the Radiant Nature of Appearances

True alchemy is not the transmutation of base metals, but the realization that all appearances emerge from the radiant, self-arising essence of awareness. When dualistic fixation dissolves and reality is directly perceived, the world is transformed. Earth becomes celestial gold, stones reveal themselves as turquoise, fire turns into water, and poison becomes ambrosia. This is the spontaneous purity of awakened vision.

In Tögal — the path of direct crossing — appearances and awareness are known to be inseparable: unified expressions of **Rigpa**, the luminous, empty, and ever-present clarity. This is not a belief, but a direct seeing, a self-certainty that arises when delusion collapses.

Tögal reveals this unity through the arising of inner light: visions spontaneously manifest, unconditioned by external causes. As **Longchenpa** wrote, "All appearances are adornments of self-radiant emptiness." In this recognition, appearances are no longer external; they are light-forms within the vast mirror of knowing.

But without recognition, these appearances become veils. A single vision can disturb the karmically entangled mind, casting it into suffering. In the hell realms, everything blazes and burns. In the world of hungry ghosts, everything is absence and craving. The six realms are not distant places, but distorted reflections of the mind, crystallizations of karmic patterns held by ignorance.

Even in ordinary experience, this is evident: in dreams, trance, fever, intoxication, or intense emotion, appearances twist. We see serpents in ropes, hear voices in silence, and mistake hallucination for truth. When illusion is taken for reality, suffering intensifies.

Shardza Tashi Gyaltsen (1859–1933/1935), the great Dzogchen adept of the Bön tradition, is said to have attained the rainbow body — dissolving his physical form into pure light. He taught that the Tögal visions — rainbows, light-rings, spheres and mandalas — are not hallucinations, but the luminous display of unobstructed awareness. Yet without proper recognition, even these can entangle the ego.

(*Self-Dawning of the Three Bodies — sku gsum rang shar —* is his profound exposition on the realization of the three kayas.) (*Commentary on Trul Khor* offers yogic instructions on the pathways of energy and awareness.)

Born in Kham, Shardza was both a realized yogi and an erudite scholar. His teachings transcended sectarian boundaries and emphasized ethical living — vegetarianism, non-harm, and integration of wisdom and conduct.

The Luminous Display of Mind

All phenomena are appearances of mind. Without recognition of their empty and luminous nature, beings wander endlessly in samsara. Not a single appearance has true solidity: all are dreams, illusions, reflections.

Who conjures these karmic visions? No one outside. It is **Rigpa**, the pure presence of awareness itself. Through it arise all experiences, all worlds, all perception.

When awareness is forgotten, the mind chases illusion and spirals into confusion. This pattern has repeated across innumerable lives, sustained by ignorance, attachment, and fear.

To those who fail to recognize the nature of mind, all appearances — however beautiful or terrifying — are like dreams within dreams, mirages dancing across the desert of samsara.

To see the mind as it is: unproduced, ungraspable, and crystal-clear — this is liberation.

Yongdzin Lopön Tenzin Namdak Rinpoche taught: "Merely knowing that appearances are illusion is not sufficient. One must directly experience how illusion liberates into wisdom."

In Tögal, this wisdom dawns through spontaneous visions: points of light, rainbow rays, spheres, and intricate mandalas — forms arising from the central channel, reflecting intrinsic awareness. These are not imagined projections, but the freeing of appearances into their luminous essence.

The *Lung Drug* scripture declares: "These forms, without base or origin, Emerge exactly in accord with one's own conception."

The Symbolic Realms of Appearance

When **Rigpa** is obscured, appearances become chains:

- Anger fuels the inferno of hell.
- Craving shapes the realm of hungry ghosts.
- Ignorance manifests as animal instinct.
- Jealousy sustains the conflict of asuras.
- Pride blooms as the blissful delusion of gods.
- Attachment binds the cycle of human birth.

These are not realms "out there," but internal states of consciousness. As **Nangzher Löpo** and **Yongdzin Rinpoche** emphasize, dreams and hallucinations mirror karmic residues projected on the canvas of awareness.

Vision as Revelation

In Tögal, there is nothing to reject or modify. Liberation arises through recognition. Practicing while gazing softly into the open sky, visions arise — lights, spheres, radiant mandalas. These are not mental fabrications, but the spontaneous dance of **Rigpa** itself. This is the secret transmission of **Padmasambhava**, entrusted to **Vairotsana** and **Yeshe Tsogyal**.

Longchenpa revealed: "These visions are like reflections — not solid, not illusory. They are the natural play of awareness, like rainbows in the sky."

This is Tögal: the realization that form is inseparable from light, and light is inseparable from mind. In this radiant clarity, appearances speak their truth: everything is already free.

Meditation, Conduct, and Sacred Commitment

View (Tibetan: ལྟ་བ་) To contemplate without extremes or conditions, as Garab Dorje taught, is to see directly the nature of mind: spacious, luminous, without origin or elaboration. It is not a theory nor a conceptual construction, but the clear and direct recognition of *rigpa*, pure awareness. > "All phenomena are the play of awareness; > Recognize them as your own face." > — Garab Dorje

Meditation (Tibetan: བསྒོམ་པ་) It is not forced effort or a cumulative technique, but undistracted resting in that view, without clinging or rejecting anything. Like a mirror that reflects without attachment; like the sky unaffected by clouds. Meditation in Dzogchen is not separate from life: every moment becomes a field of lucid presence. > "Remaining without meditating is the highest meditation." > — Longchenpa

Conduct (Tibetan: སྤྱོད་པ་) It is not based on external rules or dualistic ethical strategies. It is spontaneous action born from inner clarity—unfabricated, free of karmic intention. This is what Padmasambhava referred to as: > "Benefiting beings without creating karma" — the effortless activity of the wise, like the sun that illuminates without effort or bias. > "When the mind rests in its true nature, > action arises as effortless compassion." > — Padmasambhava

◈ **Sacred Commitment (Samaya – Tibetan: དམ་ཚིག་)** Beyond outer vows, the sacred bond in Dzogchen is natural loyalty to one's own enlightened nature. It is spontaneous communion with the master, the method, and the original mind. It is not broken by mistakes, but by forgetting the natural state. To cultivate *samaya* is to remain present, open, and trusting in the innate light. > "True samaya is to recognize and not stray from the state of rigpa." > — Vimalamitra

Shardza Tashi Gyaltsen describes this fully non-dual union in his Tögal liturgy; *where the indivisibility of emptiness and form is essential.*

Fruit, Post-Meditation, and Supreme Vision

Uncompassionate finality Turns meditation into resting. The luminous gain from samsara Becomes clear like Tögal visions. Meditation sustained in the stream of prior recognition Engages effortlessly with self-arising mind. Since meditation has become actualized, Emptiness is certain beyond it. — (Tibetan verse translated)

When Practice Matures:

The **Fruit** arises effortlessly.

In **post-meditation**, relaxation is complete.

Supreme vision unfolds as luminous appearances—verbal expressions of Tögal (lights, colors).

When practice ripens, the fruit arises naturally, like a flower opening to the sun without being forced. In the infinite stillness of the supreme equality, the mind dissolves into an ocean without waves or wind.

Silent meditation—no inertia, but pure presence—becomes a continuous flow, without beginning or end. There is no division between wakefulness and contemplation: the mind neither clings nor scatters, remaining radiant, as clear as the sky after a storm—free of contrivance, without veil or obstacle.

In the repose that follows meditation, relaxation is total: body, speech, and mind rest in their natural state, like a flawless mirror reflecting without judgment or distortion.

Then, like dawn dissolving the shadows, pure vision is revealed effortlessly—not as dream or illusion, but as the **clarity-visions of Tögal**: dancing lights, singing colors, breathing mandalas, subtle whispers of ultimate reality.

These visions do not come from outside nor from imagination—they are the **spontaneous glow of inner light**, clear and empty mind gazing upon itself in form and color, inviting us to recognize essence without grasping or aversion.

The **fruit of practice cannot be possessed**. It is not an achievement or a trophy, but the **free expression of the awakened being**, the **natural unfolding of perfect realization**.

Symbols of Realization: Sesame, Lamp, and the Imprisoned King

- **Sesame and oil**—seeds infused not in appearance but in essence—reflect how even the seeds of samsara contain awakened intention.
- **The lamp in the bowl** (form and consciousness) recalls Vimalamitra and Mañjushrimitra: **essence shines through the body**, emerging via the senses like fire rising from deep within.
- **The imprisoned king**: the two inner kings—wisdom and afflictions—rule us when wisdom is ignored. The strategy (an ambush) symbolizes **the final lotus practice (Tib. Dzokpo)** that conquers the inner enemy.

🌀 Integration with Tögal

In Tögal, these are **not metaphors**, but **lived experience**:

- You recognize the very light as **the prince restored to the throne**: vision and appearance as one.
- You see your own face in the **transparent mirror of pure vision**, unveiled.
- The **one nature**, surrounded by infinite phenomena, reveals itself as **Bella Luz**.
- **Spontaneous visions** in dreams, lucid states, peaceful apparitions or warrior forms all become **living knowledge**.

In Tögal, **direct experience transcends symbol**:

These are not just illustrations—but **real and palpable awakenings** that arise in profound practice.

You recognize the very light—**primordial luminosity**—as the prince returning to his throne: **awareness awakening to itself in its most radiant form**.

There is no split between subject and object; **vision and what appears are an indivisible unity**.

In that instant, you behold your own face reflected in the crystal mirror of clear seeing, with no veil to distort or obscure the truth.

It is not a superficial image, but **direct recognition of the essential nature**, free from illusion and falsehood.

The undivided, unfragmented nature, surrounded by the infinite play of phenomena, **reveals itself as Bella Luz**—a luminous unfolding of forms and colors that are nothing other than the **spontaneous display of the awakened mind**.

The spontaneous visions arising in dreams, lucid states that blur the line between sleep and wakefulness, gentle hallucinations of peace, or even warrior guardians—**all become living wisdom**, nonconceptual knowledge that transforms perception and everyday experience.

These are **not fantasies or illusions to be dismissed**, but gateways to profound understanding of ultimate reality—**where light and form, sleep and wakefulness, merge in the sacred dance of the awakened mind**.

As **Namkhai Norbu Rinpoche** said: > "Simply relax; let presence manifest without effort."

This is the fruit: **your luminous spontaneity, awakened and free**.

> "There is no teaching so profound that it cannot connect to your direct experience of the primordial state." > — Tenzin Wangyal Rinpoche

Epilogue – The Luminous Abiding

Dzogchen: there is nothing to attain—only revelation

In the vast sky of the Great Perfection, there is no coming, no going—only the **self-liberating brilliance of presence**. This book was not written to convince, but to remind: the Light has always been here. The path of Tögal does not add anything to who we are—it simply opens the inner eye to what has never been separate.

To recognize and rest in rigpa is to abide in **the spontaneous unfolding of the Buddhas' heart**, inseparable from our own. It is here that *samaya* finds its highest expression—not as oath, but as **unwavering trust in the purity of what we already are**. Unbroken by mistakes, sustained by remembrance.

མི་རྟོག་པར། **Mi tok par**—Impermanence—is the soft thunder that echoes beneath all appearances. Everything changes, and within that ceaseless change, the indestructible is revealed. The teachings dissolve into silence, yet the clarity they unveil is beyond all loss. It is the deep understanding of *Mitakpa* that leads us to seek refuge in the stillness of Rigpa, the one truth that does not change.. — Impermanence — is the silent song of all forms. Appearances arise and dissolve like clouds across the mirror-sky of mind. Yet in this dissolving, the unborn shines: **Rigpa**, pure presence, ungraspable and ever-radiant.

In the vast sky, there is no coming and no going—only the self-liberating brilliance of pure presence. This book was not written to persuade, but to remember: the Light has always been here. Tögal adds nothing to who we are; it simply opens the inner eye to what has never been separate from us. It is the culmination of

Dzogchen's vision, the summit of a practice that reveals the innate.

To recognize and rest in Rigpa is to dwell in the spontaneous unfolding of the Buddhas' heart, inseparable from our own. It is here that *samaya* finds its highest expression—not as a mere vow or oath, but as **an unshakable trust in the purity of what we already are**. A trust not broken by mistakes, but upheld by the simple act of remembering our true nature.

To my teachers—seen and unseen, near and far—this heart bows with gratitude. You showed the way not with words, but through your being: mirrors polished by devotion, transmission made flesh. Your breath moves through these pages, nourishing each teaching.

I bow in deep gratitude. Their gaze, their silence, their transmission beyond words has opened the pathless path. From the depths of my heart, I offer these pages as a lamp in the wind — flickering, yet lit with devotion.

And now, to you, *dear reader on the path*—

May you remember what was never lost. May your visions ripen into liberation. May your mind rest in its natural state. May the luminous fruit of Tögal blossom from within. May all beings recognize themselves in the Light that knows no other.

And in the end, which is no end, may we all awaken together, timelessly.

Rigpa remains. The sky welcomes. Now and always. 🌈□ ✨

མི་འགྱུར་མེད། *Mi gyur me yin* — It does not change. Because it was never anything else.

To those who walk the Great Perfection, may you know that your essence is stainless from the beginning. May the radiance of Tögal guide you not only to see, but to rest, to dissolve, and to abide.

May all beings swiftly recognize their true nature. May the samaya of Dzogchen remain unbroken. And in the great expanse of **mitakpa**, may we meet again — as rainbows, as space, as silence.

May all beings awaken.

Nangzher Löpo An 8th-century Bön sage, student of **Tapihritsa** and a direct holder of the *Zhang Zhung Nyen Gyü*

Biographies

A set of **inspirational short biographies** for the key Dzogchen and Bön masters you listed. Each entry focuses on their spiritual contributions, realization, and legacy in a poetic yet factual tone, suitable for inclusion in a spiritual book.

◆ Gyalwa Gyaltsen

An extraordinary master in the Bön Dzogchen lineage, a direct holder of the *Zhang Zhung Nyen Gyü*, the Oral Transmission of Zhang Zhung. Known for his unwavering devotion, depth of realization, and yogic attainment. His recognition of the natural state was so profound that his teachings became a bridge between the visible and the invisible — between appearance and essence. In deep meditative absorption, he merged into the luminous expanse of awareness, guiding others by example into the heart of self-liberation.

◆ Tapihritsa (Taphiritsa)

An 8th-century enlightened master of the Zhang Zhung Dzogchen lineage, Tapihritsa realized the rainbow body and remains accessible as an *awakened presence.* He is revered as a *vidyadhara*, a holder of pristine awareness, and is often invoked in Dzogchen meditation. To this day, he is the symbol of self-liberated mind — unborn, unceasing, and luminous.

◆ Nangzher Löpo

An 8th-century Bön sage, Aimed defending the integrity of the indigenous Dzogchen path. His realization of *Zhang Zhung Nyen Gyü* Dzogchen was profound, seeing all appearances as the display of awareness. His teachings affirm that the ultimate truth is beyond concepts, and his dialogues remain treasured in Bön texts. **Nangzher Löpo** was a brilliant scholar and accomplished practitioner. Initially a learned but skeptical intellectual, his destiny changed when he received a direct vision of the enlightened being **Tapihritsa**, who appeared in radiant form. In this sacred meeting, Tapihritsa transmitted the heart-essence of Dzogchen — the realization of *Bönku* (Dharmakāya), unconditioned awareness. This encounter shattered conceptual limitations and ignited in Nangzher Löpo the full realization of *rigpa.* He became one of the most eloquent voices of Dzogchen, composing profound commentaries and songs of liberation that continue to guide sincere practitioners into the natural state.

Zhang Zhung Nyen Gyü Lineage (Oral Transmission from Zhang Zhung) This is the oldest Dzogchen lineage in Bön, transmitted orally from master to disciple before being written down. It emphasizes direct experience and visionary transmission.

1. **Kuntu Zangpo** – Primordial Buddha
2. **Sangwa Düpa** – Sambhogakaya form who transmits the teachings
3. **Tonpa Shenrab Miwoche** – Human emanation of Kuntu Zangpo, founder of Bön
4. **Yongsu Dagpa** – Early lineage holder
5. **Tapihritsa** – Realized master who attained the rainbow body and became an immortal wisdom being
6. **Gyerpung Nangzher Löpo** – 8th-century disciple of Tapihritsa who received the teachings in visionary form and wrote them down
7. **Ponchen Tsanpo** – Translated the teachings from Zhang Zhung language into Tibetan
8. **Orgom Kundul & Yangton Sherab Gyaltsen** – Systematized the teachings in the 11th century
9. **Druchen Gyalwa Yungdrung** – 13th-century master who composed the *Gyalwa Chaktri*, a key practice manual
10. **Yongdzin Tenzin Namdak Rinpoche** – Senior living master of the lineage
11. **Tenzin Wangyal Rinpoche** – Contemporary lineage holders and teachers

This lineage has remained **unbroken and uninterrupted**, never concealed as terma, and is considered a *bka' ma* (continuous transmission)

◆**Me'u Gongdzö (1038–1096)** is credited as the founder of the A-khrid system. He received the Dzogchen teachings through the Bön lineage and systematized them into a structured meditative path. Kept by **Nyamme Sherab Gyaltsen (1356–1415)**, founder of **Menri Monastery**, helped institutionalize A-khrid within the monastic curriculum.

The system was later **codified and widely transmitted** by **Bru-sgom Gyalwa Yungdrung (1242–1290)**, a great scholar and practitioner who composed the foundational text *The Stages of A-khrid Meditation*

The **A-khrid Dzogchen lineage** (pronounced *A-tri*) is one of the three principal Dzogchen systems in the **Bön tradition**. Its name means "Guidance through the Letter A," where the white Tibetan letter ཨ symbolizes **primordial emptiness**—the unborn, unceasing nature of mind.

◆ Yongdzin Lopön Tenzin Namdak Rinpoche

The greatest living Bön Dzogchen master, born in 1926 in Khyungpo, Tibet, Yongdzin Rinpoche dedicated his life to preserving and transmitting the ancient teachings of Bön. A direct student of both oral and terma traditions, he became abbot of

Menri Monastery and later established centers in exile. His wisdom, humility, and tireless guidance have opened the door of liberation for countless beings. His teachings on *Trekchö* and *Tögal* in the Bön tradition remain unmatched in clarity.

◆ His Holiness the 33rd Menri Trizin Rinpoche (Lungtok Tenpai Nyima)

Spiritual head of the Bön tradition until his passing in 2017, the 33rd Menri Trizin was a bridge between worlds — preserving the ancient teachings while offering them in modern contexts. With deep scholarship and luminous realization, he revived the Menri lineage in India after exile and uplifted the Bön community worldwide. His compassion, presence, and laughter still resonate through his disciples.

◆ Tenzin Wangyal Rinpoche

A visionary teacher and bridge-builder between East and West, Tenzin Wangyal Rinpoche transmits the heart-essence of Bön Dzogchen with clarity and depth. Trained under Yongdzin Rinpoche, he founded Ligmincha International and brought teachings on *inner refuge*, *dream yoga*, and *Tögal visions* to a global audience. His writing and presence continue to awaken minds to their luminous nature.

◆ Garab Dorje (Prahevajra)

The first human Dzogchen master, born in Uddiyana, Garab Dorje received the Dzogchen teachings directly from the dharmakaya. He condensed all instructions into the Three Words That Strike the Vital Point. His final testament was a rainbow display of freedom. He initiated the golden lineage of direct introduction to *Rigpa*, a transmission that lives on in every true Dzogchen teaching.

◆ Manjushrimitra

Disciple of Garab Dorje and master of clarity, Manjushrimitra classified the Dzogchen teachings into *Semde*, *Longde*, and *Menngagde*. He taught the subtle distinctions between mind and awareness and passed the heart essence to Shri Singha. His name evokes the union of wisdom and compassion.

◆ Shri Singha

A luminous Indian master, Shri Singha carried the heart essence (*Menngagde*) into Tibet. He received transmissions in charnel grounds, forests, and pure visions. His teachings on the *secret instruction class* empowered the future Tibetan lineage and transmitted the *direct crossing* path, Tögal. His students included Padmasambhava, Vimalamitra, and Jnanasutra.

◆ Jnanasutra

A realized disciple of Shri Singha, Jnanasutra safeguarded the most secret instructions and passed them on to Vimalamitra. Known for penetrating wisdom, he embodied the view that nothing ever departs from Dharmakaya. In solitary retreat, he brought forth clarity like the rising sun in a cloudless sky.

◆ Vimalamitra

One of the principal Indian masters to transmit Dzogchen to Tibet, Vimalamitra brought the *Semde* and *Menngagde* lineages and remained in Tibet for many years. Through deep meditative absorption, he is said to have attained the *immortal body*. His teachings continue to shine in the Nyingma tradition as a lamp of timeless awareness.

◆ Padmasambhava (Guru Rinpoche)

The Lotus-Born Master, Padmasambhava manifested from a lotus in the land of Uddiyana and brought Vajrayāna and Dzogchen to Tibet. He subdued obstacles and concealed treasure teachings (*terma*) for future generations. His *Tögal* transmissions and teachings on dream, bardo, and liberation remain at the heart of Tibetan Buddhism. He is not just a teacher, but the living presence of awakened mind.

◆ Vairotsana

One of the first Tibetan *lotsawas* (translators), Vairotsana was a heart disciple of Padmasambhava and a direct receiver of Dzogchen teachings from Shri Singha. He traveled secretly to India and returned with radiant teachings on the Great Perfection. He became a shining light in Tibet, planting the seeds of liberation for countless beings.

Primordial Source

1. **Samantabhadra** (*Kuntuzangpo*) – The Primordial Buddha, source of all Dzogchen teachings
2. **Vajrasattva** – Sambhogakaya form who transmits the teachings to human masters

□ Indian Masters

3. **Garab Dorje** (*Prahevajra*, ~1st century CE) – First human to receive and transmit Dzogchen in Nygma tradition.
4. **Manjushrimitra** – Received the Three Statements that Strike the Essential Point
5. **Shri Singha** – Systematized the teachings into four cycles
6. **Jnanasutra** – Close disciple of Shri Singha
7. **Vimalamitra** – Brought the *Menngagde* (Instruction Class) to Tibet
8. **Padmasambhava** – Transmitted both *Semde* and *Menngagde* to Tibetan disciples
9. **Vairotsana** – One of the first Tibetan translators, trained by Shri Singha

□□ Tibetan Masters

10. **Yeshe Tsogyal** – Yogini and consort of Padmasambhava
11. **Longchen Rabjam (Longchenpa, 1308–1364)** – Codified Dzogchen view in the *Seven Treasuries*
12. **Jigme Lingpa (1730–1798)** – Revealed the *Longchen Nyingthig* cycle through visionary transmission

---

◆ Yeshe Tsogyal

The queen of yoginis, Yeshe Tsogyal was both consort and chief disciple of Padmasambhava. She realized the ultimate nature and concealed many termas for future generations. Her life of courage, devotion, and complete realization makes her a supreme example of feminine wisdom and fearless compassion.

◆ Longchen Rabjam (Longchenpa)

The omniscient Longchenpa (1308–1364) was the greatest systematizer of Dzogchen teachings. His poetic genius, depth of realization, and philosophical mastery produced the Seven Treasuries, immortal texts on the *Great Perfection.* He taught the unity of view, meditation, and conduct, and his words radiate like sunlight through the clouds of confusion.

◆ Namkhai Norbu Rinpoche

One of the foremost Dzogchen masters of modern times, Namkhai Norbu (1938–2018) brought the essence of the tradition to the world without ritual excess. Founder of the Dzogchen Community, he taught in a direct, experiential style, emphasizing presence and the natural state. His legacy of openness, clarity, and integration continues to awaken practitioners across the globe.

Jigme Lingpa (1730–1798) stands as a towering figure in the Nyingma school of Tibetan Buddhism, revered as a pivotal transmitter and innovator of the profound Dzogchen teachings. As a *tertön*—a revealer of hidden spiritual treasures (*terma*)—he unearthed and systematized the **Longchen Nyingthig** ("Heart Essence of the Vast Expanse"), a comprehensive cycle of Dzogchen instructions that rapidly became the most widely practiced and influential tradition within the Nyingma lineage. His work revitalized Dzogchen practice and profoundly shaped the spiritual landscape of Tibet.

The genesis of the Longchen Nyingthig is attributed to a series of extraordinary visionary experiences that Jigme Lingpa underwent during an extended retreat at Chimpu, near the sacred Samye Monastery. In one particularly vivid vision, he found himself miraculously transported to the great Boudhanath Stupa in Nepal. There, he was greeted by wisdom dakinis who offered him sacred scrolls and crystal beads, symbolic representations of profound Dzogchen wisdom. Upon consuming these symbolic offerings within the vision, the entirety of the Longchen Nyingthig cycle of teachings spontaneously awakened within his mind, like a seed blossoming into a full-grown tree. These visions were not mere hallucinations but direct transmissions of enlightened wisdom, a hallmark of the *terma* tradition.

Despite the immediacy and power of these revelations, Jigme Lingpa maintained a period of contemplative silence, keeping the teachings secret for several years. He only began to transcribe and transmit them publicly after receiving further visions of Longchen Rabjam (1308-1364), the illustrious 14th-century Dzogchen master whose wisdom Jigme Lingpa was believed to embody and whose teachings formed a crucial basis for the Nyingthig cycle. This connection to Longchenpa underscored the authenticity and depth of the revealed *terma*.

Beyond the Longchen Nyingthig, Jigme Lingpa's literary contributions are substantial and include the *Treasury of Precious Qualities* (Yönten Dzö), a comprehensive overview of the Buddhist path, and a monumental nine-volume history of the Nyingma school, a work of profound scholarship that helped solidify the lineage's historical and doctrinal foundations. He also played a crucial role, with the support of the royal family of Derge, in compiling and preserving the **Nyingma Gyübum**, a vast collection of rare and essential Nyingma tantras, ensuring their survival for future generations.

Jigme Lingpa's impact extended far beyond his own time. His emphasis on direct experience and the integration of profound philosophical understanding with practical application laid the groundwork for the Rimé (non-sectarian or ecumenical) movement in Tibetan Buddhism, which sought to bridge divides between different schools and emphasize shared contemplative practices. His legacy continues to inspire practitioners today, and his reincarnations are believed to include such influential figures as Patrul Rinpoche, Jamyang Khyentse Wangpo, and Dodrupchen Jigme Trinle Özer, further cementing his enduring influence on Tibetan Buddhism.

Bibliography

The following books are not directly quoted, but can provide deeper knowledge:

Bon

- *Wonders of the Natural Mind: The Essence of Dzogchen in the Native Bön Tradition of Tibet* by Tenzin Wangyal Rinpoche:

- "The Bon Religion: History, Types & Beliefs" by Study.com
- "Bon: The Ancient Religion of Tibet" by David Snellgrove
- "The Eternal Bon: The Religion of Bonpo Tibetans" by Per Kvaerne
- *Tibetan Zen: Discovering a Lost Tradition* – Sam van Schaik
- *Unearthing Bon Treasures* – Dan Martin
- *The Bon Religion of Tibet: The Iconography of a Living Tradition* – Per Kværne
- *Healing with Form, Energy, and Light* – Tenzin Wangyal Rinpoche
- *Bonpo Dzogchen Teachings* – John Myrdhin Reynolds
- *Tibetan Yoga for Health & Well-Being* – Alejandro Chaoul
- *The Great Perfection (rDzogs chen): A Philosophical and Meditative Teaching of Tibetan Buddhism* – Samten Gyaltsen Karmay

Dzogchen

- "The Natural Great Perfection" by Keith Dowman
- "The Great Perfection: A Dzogchen Teaching" by Tenzin Wangyal Rinpoche
- The Nyingma School of Tibetan Buddhism: Its Fundamentals and History – Dudjom Rinpoche
- A Marvelous Garland of Rare Gems: Biographies of Masters of Awareness in the Dzogchen Lineage – Nyoshul Khenpo
- Dzogchen: The Great Perfection – Sam van Schaik
- Dzogchen and the Path of Light – Jean-Luc Achard
- The Oral Tradition from Zhang-Zhung: An Introduction to the Bonpo Dzogchen Teachings – John Myrdhin Reynolds

Mahamudra

- "Mahamudra: The Moonlight" by Keith Dowman
- "The Practice of Mahamudra" by Chogyam Trungpa
- "The Great Path of Awakening" by Jigme Lingpa

Lama Tenzin Wangyal Rinpoche

- Awakening The Luminous Mind: Tibetan Meditation for Inner Peace and Joy
- Tibetan Sound Healing
- Awakening the Sacred Body
- The True Source of Healing: How the Ancient Tibetan Practice of Soul Retrieval Can Transform and Enrich Your Life
- Wonders of the Natural Mind: The Essence of Dzogchen in the Native Bon Tradition of Tibet

- Spontaneous Creativity: Meditations for Manifesting Your Positive Qualities
- Tibetan Yogas of Body, Speech, And Mind
- The Tibetan Yogas of Dream and Sleep: Practices for Awakening
- Unbounded Wholeness: Dzogchen, Bon, and the Logic of the Nonconceptual

Tenzin Namdak

- Twenty-One Nails Volume II: Oral commentaries by Lopon Tenzin Namdak and Tenzin Wangyal Rinpoche
- The First Experiential Transmission of the Zhang Zhung Nyam Gyu: Oral Teachings on the Ngondro: Winter Retreat Serenity Ridge December 26 - 30, 2000

Namkhai Norbu

- "The Mirror of the Sky" by Namkhai Norbu
- The Crystal and the Way of Light: Sutra, Tantra, and Dzogchen – Namkhai Norbu
- "The Practice of Dzogchen" by Namkhai Norbu

Dalai Lama

- The Art of Happiness
- The Universe in a Single Atom
- Mind of Clear Light: The Practice of Traditional Tibetan Meditation

Advaita Vedanta

- "The Bhagavad Gita" translated by Eknath Easwaran
- "The Upanishads" translated by Eknath Easwaran
- "The Principal Upanishads" by Swami Nikhilananda

Zen

- "The Complete Works of Dogen" by Dogen Zenji
- "The Three Pillars of Zen" by Philip Kapleau
- "Zen Mind, Beginner's Mind" by Shunryu Suzuki
- "The Art of Simple Living" by Shunmyo Masuno

Thich Nhat Hanh

- "The Miracle of Mindfulness" by Thich Nhat Hanh
- "Peace Is Every Step" by Thich Nhat Hanh
- "The Art of Simple Living" by Shunmyo Masuno

Taoism

- Tao Te Ching, Lao Tzu
- *Daoism: A Short Bibliography* – Fabrizio Pregadio
- *Early Daoist Scriptures* – Stephen R. Bokenkamp

- *Lao Tzu and Taoism* – Max Kaltenmark
- *Taoism: The Enduring Tradition* – Russell Kirkland
- *The Taoist Experience: An Anthology* – Livia Kohn
- *Daoism Handbook* – Livia Kohn (Editor)
- *Taoism under the T'ang: Religion and Empire during the Golden Age of Chinese History* – T. H. Barrett
- *A Survey of Taoist Literature: Tenth to Seventeenth Centuries* – Judith M. Boltz
- *Taoïsme et corps humain: Le Xiuzhen tu* – Catherine Despeux
- *Taoist Ritual in Chinese Society and History* – John Lagerwey
- *Tao Te Ching* – D. C. Lau
- *Taoism and the Arts of China* – Stephen Little & Shawn Eichman
- *The Encyclopedia of Taoism* – Fabrizio Pregadio (Editor)
- *Taoism: Growth of a Religion* – Isabelle Robinet
- *The Taoist Body* – Kristofer Schipper
- *The Taoist Canon: A Historical Companion to the Daozang* – Kristofer Schipper & Franciscus Verellen (Editors)
- *Chronicle of Taoist Studies in the West 1950-1990* – Anna Seidel
- *La divinisation de Lao tseu dans le Taoïsme des Han* – Anna Seidel
- *Taoism: The Unofficial High Religion of China* – Anna Seidel
- *Religious Taoism and Popular Religion from the Second to Seventh Centuries* – Rolf A. Stein
- *The Complete Works of Chuang Tzu* – Burton Watson
- *Taoism: An Essential Guide* – Eva Wong

The Autor

Tagzig, Eustaquio Martínez del Río:

A Visionary in Art, Spirituality, and Human Potential

The Autor
Tagzig (Eustaquio Martinez del Rio):

A Luminary on the Path of Consciousness, Creativity, and Global Awakening

Tagzig, known formally as Eustaquio Martinez del Rio, stands as a distinguished figure whose life journey epitomizes the profound integration of spiritual wisdom, artistic expression, and a deep commitment to global well-being. A polymath whose expertise spans meditation teaching, writing, film direction, photography, and ecology, Tagzig's work consistently explores the intricate nexus of mystical, spiritual, ecological, and social themes, guiding audiences and readers toward introspection and positive transformation.

Born in Mexico City, Tagzig's early life was profoundly shaped by the devout Catholic faith of his grandparents and the rich spiritual inclinations of his immediate family. These foundational experiences instilled in him a timeless ethical framework, which he perceives as illuminating humanity's inherent goodness and fostering societal harmony from a "celestial essence." His father, a business advisor, introduced him to the transformative power of Buddhist meditation and neurolinguistic wisdom, expanding his perception beyond conventional paradigms and guiding him toward an ever-expanding consciousness and an open heart capable of perceiving subtle realms. His mother, a gifted psychologist, provided a grounding in joyful creativity, intellectual brilliance, and culinary artistry.

A pivotal moment in Tagzig's formative years arose paradoxically from financial dissolution. This challenging period led his family to embark on a "sacred retreat"—a camping experience in an ancient forest by crystalline waters. Here, facing frost-kissed dawns, his father introduced spiritual challenges, including immersion in frigid waters. At a tender age, Tagzig embraced this rigorous initiation, traversing the dock's length to surrender to the icy embrace before swimming swiftly shoreward. Such experiences, he recounts, fortified his inner strength, divine will, and an understanding of unlimited potential. This early training instilled in him the profound wisdom of maintaining humble receptivity and embracing infinite possibilities, which became a cornerstone of his evolving consciousness. Through deep contemplation, he discovered that belief in possibility inherently manifests reality, while resistance merely obscures divine opportunities.

Tagzig's personal odyssey has been marked by the transcendence of significant challenges, including dyslexia, social integration difficulties, physical trials, and profound losses. During intense spiritual testing, a profound insight was shared with him: "Limitations exist solely within mind's confines; beyond lies infinite possibility." This revelation underscored the dual nature of consciousness as either a "divine ally or shadow adversary," particularly in confronting the "monkey mind" that fabricates illusory obstacles until mastered through dedicated spiritual practice. Upon achieving such mastery, the mind transforms from a master into a useful instrument of universal expression, a state exemplified by enlightened athletes, philosophers, mystics, and storytellers who channel consciousness's infinite potential.

His spiritual education commenced remarkably early. At the age of eleven, guided by his father's outstanding teachings, he successfully traversed burning coals through the art of firewalking, blending neurolinguistic wisdom with shamanic traditions. At fourteen, his spiritual journey deepened profoundly upon meeting his revered Tibetan teacher, Tenzin Wangyal Rinpoche. While pursuing film studies in England, he received divine guidance from Lama Khemsar Rinpoche, under whom he studied for five years. His immersion in Tibetan studies continued at the Manjushri Institute in Darjeeling, India, where he lived in a sacred Buddhist sanctuary. Tagzig's spiritual path has further broadened through the integration of ancestral wisdom from Mexico and

North America, interweaving with Eastern philosophies (Taoism, Buddhism) and the mystical depths of Middle Eastern Sufism. The illuminated presence of Lopon Trine Nyma Rinpoche, who guided the largest Tibetan Bon Buddhist monastery, offered profound insights into the mind's true nature through his eternal wisdom: "Place your mind behind." Having undergone countless sacred retreats and devoted meditation practice, Tagzig humbly serves as a vessel for divine wisdom, embodying the sacred responsibility of sharing these celestial teachings.

Academically and professionally, Tagzig's trajectory is equally distinguished by its breadth and depth. His educational journey includes English studies at LSI, Cambridge UK, and Filmmaking at the University of Westminster in London. His passion for the visual arts led him to photography studies at the Plymouth College of Art and specialization in writing, production, and cinematography at King's College. Further cementing his expertise, he completed a Master's degree in Cinematographic Direction and Environmental Studies from the European University Campus, Universidad Rey Juan Carlos in Spain.

Tagzig's professional career commenced with work at esteemed international companies such as Paramount Pictures and Robert Evans Company in the United States, and New Line Pictures, Hallmark Channel, and BBC Documentaries in the United Kingdom. Returning to Mexico, he founded two influential production companies, Spiritual Planet and Sidi Media, through which he has directed and produced commercials, TV series, and short films.

Between 2010 and 2012, Tagzig directed a notable series of documentary feature films, including "Mayan Codes," "México: El poder del universo," "Beyond 2012," "El sexto sol," and "Luz de mi vida Madre Teresa de Calcuta." His documentary "Buda's Smile/La Sonrisa de Buda," exploring happiness and meditative techniques, was distributed through the Blockbuster chain. His work gained significant recognition, with "Démosle una oportunidad a la Tierra" (2013) receiving acclaim at the International Human Rights Film Festival, and his short film "Memorias verdes" (2015) being selected for the Awareness Festival. "Teoría del caos" participated in the V Encuentro Hispanoamericano de Cine y Video Documental Independiente. His feature film "YACUNA" received Best Photography at the EUROFILM Festival 2016 and was later exhibited at the National Museum of History and Anthropology, Mexico (2018), before traveling across five continents. His socially conscious film "DESOLATE," focusing on a single mother, garnered the Merit of Conscience award in Los Angeles, USA. In 2022, he directed and produced the romantic comedy "HAPPY FOREVER." His dedication to global well-being is further exemplified by his collaboration with the United Nations to produce the "City Children and Smart Cities" documentary, alongside studies at The SDG Academy, U.S.A., and Columbia University on storytelling for social change and achieving the Sustainable Development Goals.

As an author, Tagzig continues to disseminate his profound insights. His published works include:

- *A Gift for Your Life; Words that inspire, reorient, evoke reflections and cheer the soul.*
- *Simple, Deep and Happy Meditation; Discover peace in each breath, "A practical guide to enlightenment, that will transform your life."*
- *The Art of Fulfilment; the keys to personal fulfilment.*
- *The Treasure of Habits that transform life and art of fullness.*
- *Dawn of the East and Spiritual Path.*
- *Symphony of Mysticism, Spontaneous Enlightenment, inspired in non duality.*
- *The Luminous Field*

- *Mind Like a Still Lake*
- *21 pointers of The Luminous Expanse*
- *Vast and Radiant ' Symphony*
- *Clarity in the Void*

Anticipated forthcoming publications include *The Art of Sacred Sexuality*, *Dreams and Good Sleep; Rest and Mystical Journey in Life, Love, Feel and Communicate; Relationships that Lead You to Fullness*, *The Book of Contemporary Spiritual Letters*, and *Sustainable Finance to Avoid Disaster.*

Tagzig's journey reflects how his teachers illuminated the pathways of consciousness, enabling him to manifest his dreams through global pilgrimages and the creation of films that honor ancestral wisdom while nurturing social and ecological awakening. Within the sacred stillness of his mind, he discovered an infinite cosmic expanse, where worldly chaos dissolves like morning mist beneath radiant solar consciousness. Meditation revealed the subtle vibrations of present moment awareness, teaching him to dwell in the "eternal now" with divine gratitude and crystalline clarity. Where anxiety's labyrinth once clouded his vision, he now perceives existence through awakened eyes, as an infinite space of divine possibility, with each breath serving as a reminder that tranquility embodies fullness rather than emptiness, wherein he has discovered his eternal anchor, divine guide, and sacred home. His life and work serve as an inspirational testament to the power of transcending environmental limitations through unwavering faith in infinite potential, urging all to manifest their destiny.

Wosel

Instagram: eustaquiodelrio

Facebook: woselnet

Youtube: novaspiritfilms

eustaquio@sidimedia.com

ceo@wosel.com

Wosel.com - Sidimedia.com - eustaquiodelrio.com

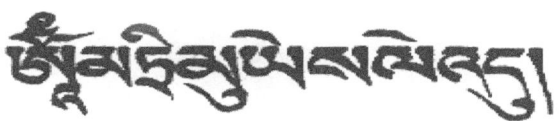

ཨོཾམཏྲིམུཡེསལེའདུ།

www.ingramcontent.com/pod-product-compliance
Lightning Source LLC
Chambersburg PA
CBHW070935180426
43192CB00039B/2212
* 9 7 8 1 9 6 6 6 8 0 1 0 9 *